My Search for Prayers that Satan Hates

This book is a winner! It reminds me of "The Shack"--a national best selling religious book that swept across America. Satan will also hate this book! It shows the power of prayer in all situations. You will be shocked with the spiritual warfare battles with Satan! You will encounter stories from people today that are beyond belief!! You will learn powerful prayer solutions that will leave you with gratefulness for God's faithfulness and protection.

*Ray Fulenwider, Retired Christian minister
and author of best selling books:
"The Prayer Driven Church" and "The Servant Driven Church."*

My Search for Prayers Satan Hates" will challenge you to take the spiritual dimension of life more seriously while giving you the tools you need to experience God's protection and direction in your daily life. Satan may hate Steve's book, but you will love it.

*Gordon Dabbs, Ph.D, Preaching Minister,
Prestoncrest Church of Christ, Dallas, TX.*

This book is a "must read" for anyone interested in being challenged to pray and "fight the good fight" Paul referred to in 1 Timothy 1:18. Steve shares a message from his life. This is a book about prayer and spiritual warfare; not in theory, but reality. He sets forth a pattern of prayers that will defeat Satan on many fronts. The examples shared are compelling and challenging. There are prayers that Satan hates. I highly recommend this book.

*Jim Woodell, Executive Director, River City Ministry,
North Little Rock, AR, and author of "Heaven's Star."*

Are evil spirits real? Do we really have an unseen enemy? Steve Hemphill says, "Yes!" Follow him on a Scriptural journey that examines how a believer can overcome the forces of darkness through prayer and the power of God's word. Marvel at the way he has seen God work to overthrow strongholds and change lives. Learn about Steve's personal experiences in spiritual warfare, and enjoy the testimony of others. You'll be blessed!

Buddy Helms, Pastor, Brentwood Family Fellowship, San Angelo, Texas, and author of "Marriage: What's the Big Deal?," "Outrageous Christian Discipleship," and "A Campaign For Christ."

Steve Hemphill has written a different book on the topic of prayer. Those who read this book and put its principles in their life will become greater "Prayer Warriors." When we call on God, we reach out to the greatest power in the universe. This book is a great read!

Coach Wally Bullington, Athletic Director Emeritus, Abilene Christian University.

As one who has experienced firsthand the horror of combat during two tours in the jungles of Vietnam, I can attest to the fact that warfare is a shock to every aspect of one's being. Yet, as Christian warriors engaged in a vast spiritual struggle with the forces of darkness, the shock is no less intense. Steve Hemphill, in this powerful new book, has provided us insight into one of the most powerful weapons at our disposal in this cosmic conflict: prayer. In so doing, he gives our fellow combatants the courage to fight on, and puts the enemy, Satan, on notice that his days are numbered. It is a must read for all who daily face the shocking subtleties of an enemy who seeks our defeat. I highly recommend it to my fellow brothers-in-arms.

Al Maxey, author of, "Down, But Not Out," "One Bread, One Body," and "Immersed By One Spirit."

Like Keyser Soze, the greatest trick the Devil ever pulled was convincing the world he didn't exist. Steve Hemphill knows that the Devil does exist, and that one of the Christian's most effective weapons in our war against him is prayer. If you are weary of fighting a defensive police action and are ready to take the battle to the enemy, pick up this book and read it. You may never be the same.

Chuck Monan, Preaching Minister,
Pleasant Valley Church of Christ, Little Rock, AR.

Anyone who is privileged to read this powerful account of Steve Hemphill's coming face to face with the prayers Satan hates will become not only fully informed but also greatly inspired to take up the Sword of the Spirit each day throughout a lifetime of service to others.

Bob Hunter, Senior Vice president Emeritus of Abilene Christian
University, & Texas State Representative 1986 - 2006.

"Lord, thank you for opening my eyes to where the true battle is." This quote is from Steve Hemphill's new book, My Search for Prayers Satan Hates. Certainly, Satan hates this prayer. Even though I have preached and taught on the subject of prayer for years, I needed to read that prayer today, and then pray it. I am thankful for this book, and thankful for this Godly man who has yielded to God's Spirit to write it. This book is a blessing already. May God use it where He wants.

David Mathews, Co-Founder and Executive
Director of Spark of Life Foundation.

The subject of spiritual warfare is one of the most important studies for this generation. The claim of those who would have us believe the darker powers of this world are greatest of all is wrong. Steve Hemphill guides us through a systematic and practical way of fighting Spiritual Warfare with the use of the Sword of the Spirit (the Word of God) and prayer. Never before have I seen such a practical approach to using prayer to fight the devil on a daily basis. Filled with specific illustrations (both from his own personal life and the life of others with whom he has communicated) it gives the admonition of Paul to "pray without ceasing" (1 Thess. 5:17) a new understanding. Some illustrations may seem difficult to accept, even far-fetched for the person who has never fought spiritual warfare at this level, but in each example he gives biblical evidence for the principle he employs.

I talk with people regularly who are fighting these kinds of battles and I believe they will be served quite well in reading Steve's book. Before you dismiss too quickly what he is saying, observe the battles that are being fought by people you know. Ask them how they are handling the forces of evil that challenge their living for Christ. You just might find yourself wanting to give them this book to read for practical help in addressing the problem.

Here is a tool of great value in helping people through the distresses of life and assuring them that God talks with us (through Scripture) and we talk to Him (through prayer) – this is the only way we will ever win the battle.

Edward P. Myers, Ph.D., Professor of Bible and Christian Doctrine, College of Bible and Ministry, Harding University

The world of unseen spirits--good and bad--does exist. Steve Hemphill, in his distinctive and forthright style, forces us to come to grips with this spiritual reality found throughout the pages of Scripture. Whether you agree with him or not, you will find yourself grappling with the concepts Steve brings the reader in his stories. A good and thought-provoking read.

Royce Money, Ph.D., Chancellor, Abilene Christian University

There is an invisible war taking place between the dominion of God and evil. If you are a Christian, there is no escaping the battle. The battle is fought every time we decide to do what is right or wrong. Satan brings this battle into our homes through media. I believe Steve Hemphill has provided a wonderful resource to encourage believers to emerge victorious in the fight. My Search for Prayers Satan Hates is a common sense look at the Bible verses that guide your spiritual warfare. He offers practical illustrations that will renew your faith in the power of prayer. This book will help equip you for the daily battle each of us face.

Noel Whitlock, Preaching Minister,
College Church of Christ, Searcy, AR

Some Christians accept fantastic stories of spiritual encounters on the mission field but struggle to believe that God (or the devil) is so active in America. Steve's personal narrative backed by extensive Scripture references may help them to think otherwise. The God of Hosts still fights for the souls of men--read this book and join Him.

Phillip Shero, Vice Chancellor of LivingStone
International University

my search *for*

Prayers Satan Hates

Steve Hemphill

my search *for*

Prayers Satan Hates

TATE PUBLISHING
AND **ENTERPRISES**, LLC

Published by Tate Publishing & Enterprises, LLC
127 E. Trade Center Terrace | Mustang, Oklahoma 73064 USA
1.888.361.9473 | www.tatepublishing.com

Tate Publishing is committed to excellence in the publishing industry. The company reflects the philosophy established by the founders, based on Psalm 68:11,
"The Lord gave the word and great was the company of those who published it."

Book design copyright © 2013 by Tate Publishing, LLC. All rights reserved.
Cover design by Errol Villamante
Interior design by Caypeeline Casas

Published in the United States of America

ISBN: 978-1-62746-229-7
1. Religion / Christian Life / Prayer
2. Religion / Christian Life / Spiritual Warfare
13.10.02

Acknowledgements

First, I want to acknowledge and thank my wife, Mary Lynn Spencer Hemphill for putting up with me all these years. As I write this, our 34th anniversary is coming up. I'm sort of a numbers guy, and this 3 and 4 adds up to 7, a special number to God. Also, I was born on 7-27-57, which is a birthday with three 7s in it, and the 5 and 2 also add up to 7. I have always felt like a very blessed man. Thanks, Babe, for seeing me through all the tough times.

Next, I want to acknowledge and thank Jay Knight. Jay was my long-time partner at our business, and we enjoyed many morning discussions about God and the Bible while sipping a cup of coffee. (It's the one thing I have missed most after selling my company stock to him.) It was one of these talks when Jay recommended Frank Peretti's book to me.

So I also want to acknowledge and thank Frank Peretti— though I have never met him personally. Although I have enjoyed many of his books, it was Frank's first book, "This Present Darkness," that got me on the path to reading. I hated reading, and only read whatever I absolutely had to—until Jay told me about that book. It changed the course of my life. Thank you, Frank, for personifying spiritual warfare in such a compelling way. You caused me to start my own research.

Next I want to acknowledge the work, research, thought process, and life experiences of Joe Beam. His book, "Seeing the Unseen," revealed how Frank Peretti's fictional work looks in the real world. You will never know what you have done for me.

Also, I want to thank and acknowledge my mentor and good friend, Chuck Duvall, and his lovely wife Joyce. Chuck and Joyce are true encouragers. You both remind me of family, and I think of you as such. And Chuck, thank you for reviewing this work and suggesting some invaluable additions. Your wisdom and insight is inspiring.

I can't thank all these others without mentioning Ron Hutchison. Ron, you have been a rock of encouragement and support for me when no one else would. I love our walks and spiritual discussions. Your friendship is more valuable than gold. I hope to get in the same nursing home as you one day—so I can pull all sorts of pranks on you. But then … you'll probably own it and have me kicked out.

Finally, I want to think you readers. God gave me the dream of becoming a writer when I wasn't even looking for it, and it has been an exciting ride, but you guys—you who buy and read the books—you make the dream a reality. I guess I have to admit that when I first became a published author is made me want to sell a bunch of books, but when I starting hearing from readers about how my words encouraged them, inspired them, or comforted them, everything changed. Money didn't matter anymore. People did. Sure, I still have bills, kids in school, and various earthly things to pay for, but I finally started to understand God meant what He said:

> "Seek first his kingdom and his righteousness, and all these things will be given to you as well."
>
> Matthew 6:33 (NIV)

And daily life has never been the same since. I pray the same thing for you!

Dear God, please bless everyone who reads or hears the words of this book. Bless them greatly through my feeble words. Open their eyes to exactly what You want them to gain. May it encourage them, prepare them, and give them endurance to finish strong. In Jesus Name, Amen.

Foreword

At the end of the day, each of us generally will describe it as either a good day or a bad day depending on how the events we experienced impacted us. When asked to expound more, it becomes a discussion where we provide details of situations, issues, and activities throughout our day that possibly resulted in everything between successful and excruciating. However, if we are asked why these challenging things happened or how we are going to address them going forward, the conversation can easily become very short, or there is no further discussion at all, and we quickly change the subject. We hear and read about so many terrible events that occur around the world as well as in our own backyard and wonder…why? Without any understanding or plan as to how to handle the struggles we face, life can be very challenging and cause us great pain.

Have you ever considered the many forces that are around us every day that we are battling with and we can't even see them? Have you ever wondered if there was a way to see things clearer within your life each day or to have more confidence in where your daily walk was taking you? If we do not know where we are going when we get up each day, how do we know if we are taking the right pathway or not? Have you ever had someone or something influence you in a way that took you down a road that you knew was not good for you, but for some reason, you were not able to see how to change your direction or if you were, you didn't understand why you couldn't change? What if you could have someone to go to that is able and willing to provide answers, comfort, strength and hope when it all seems so confusing?

There is a powerful source that each of us has access to every second of every day. Steve will share that with us and take us on a journey into the realms of spiritual warfare in *My Search for the*

13

Prayers Satan Hates. He will take our hand and walk us through the scriptures within God's Word and help each of us see how the battle around us cannot be ignored. This book will provide vivid pictures from God's Word that clearly display that if we are not prepared each day, we can easily be misled and begin to stray from our Christian walk of faith. Satan is working every second to deceive us and striving to lead us down a path that causes great pain. Steve will describe for us why we must clearly understand that as in any battle, armor is needed for protection and that in our daily life we are also soldiers and need our complete array of armor as well to protect us from Satan. Along with our protective garments, we will read about our personal connection with our Lord and Savior as He provides us the avenue of prayer to God that gives us our daily strength.

Steve brings to us the difficult realization of the spiritual warfare we all face as he uses life stories of individuals who have endured the devious plans that Satan rolled out across their lives and then the beauty of how they were victorious. With the foundation of God's Word, Steve guides us through the power that prayer provides to each of us and for those that we love. He also encourages us by sharing the many ways that God's promise of good overcoming evil is displayed every day by people reaching out to others who are being swallowed up in their own battles and then discovering the peace within and the victory from God that comes through the power of prayer.

My Search for the Prayers Satan Hates will draw you closer to God and His power as well as raise your awareness that we need to always keep our spiritual radar on the highest level possible. If you have experienced struggles and they are still weighing on you or you are in the midst of a difficult time in your life right now, then you will be uplifted as you read about God's love for you, His protection for you and the strength He has available for you at this very moment. For those who have family or friends who have lost hope in life or have been beaten down so far they see no possibility of anything good ever happening again in their future, Steve wrote this book for you. Steve will share with you the wonder of God and His great power that can build anyone up, as he has done since the beginning of time, and guide them towards a new path that is full of hope, happiness and love.

Steve truly desires that we all seriously understand the never-ending warfare that is surrounding us with Satan and his forces, but more importantly that God is in complete control. His love for the Word of God is clearly seen in every page as he speaks to us in a powerful way, yet it feels like we are sitting in his living room and just talking about life.

As you read this book, Steve will help you see that when we place our lives in God's hands, we will be fully equipped to better understand struggles and challenges and to become a warrior for Christ, a soldier against Satan's spiritual warfare and a safe beacon to others in need.

Steve Hemphill has committed his life to sharing the beautiful message from God's Word and encouraging people to have a deeper relationship with Him. I am confident that you will see that in every page of this book.

I am richly blessed to be able to call him my friend. I pray that God will touch your heart as you read this book. May He give you the strength you seek so that you can stand firm in His Word within this world and receive the daily comfort of His love as you follow the pathway of life.

"I can do all things through Christ who strengthens me."
Philippians 4:13 (NKJV)

Steven E. Croft, Elder,
Legacy Church of Christ, Fort Worth, TX

Beginning Thoughts

Before We Begin

"Don't be *surprised* at this: A time is coming when all who are dead and in their graves will hear his voice."

John 5:28 (NCV)

Have you ever been totally surprised at something you found in the Bible? I have—repeatedly. I have often heard people say "I didn't know that was in the Bible!" If you will just open it up and read it regularly, you'll be shocked at what's in there. And some of you are going to be totally shocked and blown away with some of the thoughts and verses I have to discuss in this book. So hold on to your hat.

Before we begin, I want to say up front that this book is not rated *G*. In fact, parts of it aren't even rated *PG-13*. Some of this material is shocking, bordering on unbelievable. In order for you, dear reader, to be able to accept it as compatible with Scriptural truth and real in our world today, I must lay the foundation from God's Holy Word, the Bible. I have gone to great measures to do that.

I am also fully aware of the propensity of some to browse the chapter sections and jump forward to what they perceive to be the heart of the matter and the core of the thoughts I am presenting here. I ask you from the bottom of my heart not to do this. Please restrain yourself to read it in the order it is presented. In fact, I would even go so far as to ask that if you are unwilling to do this, then please put this book back on the shelf and buy another one instead. I would rather you not read it at all than to jump to a section without the preface of biblical truth as a filter to see it through.

In this work I share many personal stories of spiritual warfare and many stories from others. Some are shocking, seemingly too fantastic to be true—yet I present them as truth.

In my previous work, *My Search for the Real Heaven*, I ended each chapter with a short fictional segment called, "What Might Be." This was meant to be received by the reader as an avenue of fictionally presenting one possible way heaven might be, based on the Scriptures presented in that section. One day I got a call from a fine Christian man who indicated he loved the book, but didn't agree 100 percent with a particular conclusion. I politely thanked him for his feedback but quickly reminded him that the idea he mentioned was not in the biblical study part; it was in one of these fictional endings. He was surprised, and had no recollection of this. In a way, I found that thrilling, but it was also frustrating, since he was using this idea as a criticism of my work. However, no harm, no foul, because he was actually happy and relieved to be reminded that I was only presenting that as a possibility rather than stating it as a Bible truth. There is a difference.

I think it's unfair to judge a book by it's cover, or to reject the diligent work of any author without a) reading the work in the order it's presented, or b) reading the whole thing. I thank you in advance for complying with this request.

One more thing: I prayed and prayed about how to put this book together. I asked God for wisdom, inspiration, revelation, direction, and the lead of His Spirit through the process. I didn't just want to write a book to make money; I wanted it to make a difference. I wanted it to help people and help enlarge the kingdom.

As I began to put the sequence together and the order of the things I felt led to cover here, it suddenly became apparent to me that it would be more practical and helpful to those who read it (or hear it read) if I began each section with a verse to introduce the idea about to be discussed, and then ended each section with a prayer. The prayer would do two things: 1) the prayer would reveal the motives of my heart (we don't lie to God in our prayers, right?) and focus on bringing the section to a logical, biblical, and practical conclusion, and 2) the prayer would give the readers samples of real prayers for real people in real life that are useful, encouraging, and thought provoking. In light of this, and knowing my goals for this were offered from this sort of motive, let me apologize up front if any prayer—or any phrase in any prayer—offends anyone in any way. I meant no harm, only good. Please see them through this filter; even if I am at times misguided and wrong.

Lord, I pray for a special blessing to be given to every person who buys and reads this book. Help them to use this knowledge and insight to Your glory. Open their eyes to how they can use this to pray more effectively and to serve You better and better. In Jesus's name, amen.

Writing About Spiritual Warfare is Dangerous

"Be careful of false prophets. They come to you looking gentle like sheep, but they are really *dangerous* like wolves."

Matthew 7:15 (NCV)

As my first book, *My Search for the Real Heaven*, began to fill my speaking schedule, I called my editor one day and said "I think I know what I want to write about in my next book: 'Spiritual Warfare.'" She encouraged me in this endeavor, and I didn't think much more about it.

That was on a Friday. Our youngest son, Jay, had just left for college, leaving us in the category of "empty nesters." Now I know that I lot of parents are excited by the exit from home of the youngest child, but we weren't really happy about that. We really enjoyed our children as well as their friends. We had a game room built over the garage when the boys were small, because we wanted our house to be the fun place; we wanted our children's friends to want to come over and encouraged them to invite them all the time. (That way, you always know who they're with and what they're doing, right?)

Anyway, Jay's departure left us feeling a little lonely and dejected, so Mary Lynn and I decided that Friday to go to a funny movie together to get our mind off the fact that Spencer, Blake, and Jay were all gone from home now. We needed a little cheering up.

At this point in my life as an author, I still owned my technology company and was quite busy with work, family, and business, not the least of which was helping Jay get everything he needed ready to depart for college. Suffice it to say that although I had done several exciting book signings in the previous two weeks, I hadn't had the time to run the cash deposit by the bank as I had intended that day. In fact, I forgot about it completely. There was about $5,000 in a bright blue bank bag in the back seat of my Jeep.

Lord, what I'm about to share in this book puts me and my family in spiritual danger. I pray for Your protection and for that protection to be extended to each person who reads this and puts into practice in their daily life. In Jesus's name, amen.

At the Movie

While we were in the movie—trying to laugh in order to keep from crying about our empty nest—there was a police car patrolling the small parking lot. We also took comfort in the fact that we had parked just two cars down from the sidewalk leading a short distance to the entrance and that we had parked right under a security light. But it wasn't enough.

Everything looked fine as we got back in the Jeep and buckled up, but horror took over when I turned my head to back safely out—the back window on the passenger side was gone. I froze.

Then I looked down at the items still in the back seat: books, a Bible, some folders, and an expensive camera—all still there. That led me to the incorrect conclusion that the police car must have come along at just the right moment to scare away the offender before anything went missing. But it was not to be. As I quickly took inventory—in a mild state of shock—it dawned on me that the blue bank bag was nowhere to be found. Panic rose in my throat as I remembered how much was actually in the pouch, and the fact that I hadn't made it to the bank that day.

Then it hit me—it wasn't an accident that it occurred on the very day I had informed my editor what I wanted to write about now: spiritual warfare. Satan and his forces were not happy, and they were sending me a message.

Lord, thank You for all those who have prayed for Your protection of me and my family during the researching and writing of this book. I pray it brings great glory to Your church and Your Kingdom. In Jesus's name, amen.

Encouragement

When my dad died in the summer of 2000, I heard from many people what an encouragement he was to them. One Hispanic lady said that my dad encouraged her to go to college, and she was the very first Hispanic girl from Mason, TX to attend a university. Another told me they had started a business based solely on my dad's encouragement that they could be very successful, and he had been right. Dad helped others set up their family trust funds, or helped them acquire land at a good price—the list of kind acts Dad had performed for others at no charge went on and on. Many tried to pay him, but he repeatedly refused the money, though it wasn't because our family didn't need it.

As these stories, and other like them, began to come to light, I realized that Dad hadn't just been my source of encouragement— it was a lifestyle for him. He encouraged everyone. Every day. My epiphany of this truth made me want to do that same thing for others, so I started a simple little web site called PrayerThoughts. com.

Initially, a few friends signed up, then a few more, and before long they were telling others or forwarding my daily additions. I wanted to use this to encourage others, just like Dad had encouraged me and everyone else he knew. In a fairly short time I had a few hundred subscribers. Obviously it was free, but it was also targeting men to some degree because we men often don't read enough. So it was short, to the point, and a little bit fun. Each "Prayer Thought" focuses on a Bible verse, enlarging the words from that verse that I am trying to emphasize and focus on. It also includes an insight I have personally observed or learned during my lifetime about that verse, a graphic that helps illustrate it, and a prayer that applies to it.

During my seven-year research of heaven for my first book, I invented my own color-coding system for what I consider the major themes in the Bible, so I soon began to include color-coded insights on the Prayer Thoughts verses that apply to each verse. Black is used for insights on God and His nature, brown for covenant insights, red for sin and spiritual warfare, green for prophecy, blue for heaven and angels, purple for water baptism, orange for creation and evolution, grey for biblical insights on women in Scripture, and burgundy for pointing out the literal nature of the Bible. It's sort of like putting a huge puzzle together—great fun!

This is the prayer I prayed as I began my research throughout the Scriptures on the topic of heaven:

> *Lord, You know what You meant when You wrote this; help me to know what You mean as I read it. In Jesus's name, amen.*

The Need for Prayer

For years I put out new Prayer Thoughts several times a week. At first I got a few responses, occasionally from subscribers telling me that my thought that day was really what they needed, but these kind responses dwindled to a trickle, then into oblivion. I felt at first like I was really helping people, being a source of encouragement to them, which is what my goal was in the beginning, but as the kind notes vanished, I decided no one was benefitting anymore, and that it was a waste of time to continue. So I told a close friend about my decision to discontinue and disband Prayer Thoughts.

"Hold on," he said, "before you do that let me put some tracking software in place to see how many hits it's getting."

"Okay," I replied, "I'll go a little longer and let you check that out."

"Do not despise these small beginnings, for the Lord rejoices to see the work begin."

Zechariah 4:10

It was often getting as many as a quarter of a million hits a month from almost one hundred countries. Wow. I had no idea. So I decided to continue. (You can sign up free at www. PrayerThoughts.com, or just visit the site and browse it at your leisure.) It now literally has thousands of pages, and my lifetime goal for it is to put the whole Bible in this format. I have even talked to one of my sons about continuing this work after I am gone on to my eternal reward if I don't finish it.

One of my subscribers and supporters is Billy Hibbs, Jr., a business associate in Tyler, TX who owns an insurance company called Hibbs, Hallmark, & Company. He insured my technology company for over twenty-five years and became a good friend and source of personal encouragement to me. Billy often sent me thankful feedback over particular Prayer Thoughts, posing additional questions concerning the various verses and topics presented. In a kind, joking way, he began to call me the Bible answer man.

After the $5,000 loss, I initially contacted Billy's agent, who handled the details of our policy, asking about the possibility of reimbursement. I was quickly informed that cash wasn't normally covered, since the amount was often difficult to prove, and that companies who dealt in cash had to purchase a special rider dealing with this sort of unusual and special circumstance.

Obviously, I was disappointed but tried to tell myself that God was good and that He would take care of me through this crisis, just as He had through so many others. But in the back of my mind, I was hearing, "Wow, this is a terrible time to lose $5,000, with three boys in Christian college that year." (Spencer was getting a master's in accounting at Abilene Christian University, while Blake and Jay were sophomore and freshman at Harding University, both as pre-dental students.) "Just trust God," I kept telling myself—over and over and over.

In desperation, I sent Billy an e-mail detailing my dilemma and asking him to check on it for me if possible. I got a chuckle when he did so by sending an email to one of his employees to double-check the policy for me, and added, "Now be nice to Steve, because he sends out those Prayer Thoughts each day that I enjoy so much about many Bible verses, so lightning might strike you if you don't do the right thing for him."

Basically I had given up hope on getting reimbursed when I got a phone call from one of the ladies at HHC. "Hi, Steve," she began, "we pulled your policy, and you did have the rider that covered cash, so how much do we owe you?"

I said "Five thousand," and it made my day. God is still on the throne!

This whole event led me to an important deduction: if I am going to write about spiritual warfare, I'm going to need some prayer warriors to pray for me on a regular basis.

"My dear children, you belong to God and have defeated them; because God's Spirit, who is in you, is greater than the **devil**, who is in the world."

1 John 4:4 (NCV)

Lord, thank you for seeing that I was reimbursed for my stupidity during this transitional time in my life of service to You. Thank You for Your patience with me as I continue to learn and grow closer to You each day. When I am delivered from each new crisis, remind me that it's You doing it. In Jesus's name, amen.

Ephesians Chapter 6

Poem Prayer for Today

Father, help me start each day,
Talking to You; Seeking YOUR way,
Tune my heart to hear Your voice,
Help me as I make each choice.
Help my mind to see your plan,
Give me strength to know I can.
Open my eyes to see Your ways,
Help me to be faithful all my days.

Lord, help me to always start each new day with a prayer; seeking Your input on all my plans and decisions. I pray that my life brings you glory: every response, every example, every decision, and every moment. In Jesus's name, amen.

It's War

"Put on all of God's *armor* so that you will be able to stand firm against all strategies of the devil. For we are not fighting against flesh-and-blood enemies, but against evil rulers and authorities of the unseen world, against mighty powers in this dark world, and against evil spirits in the heavenly places."

Ephesians 6:11-12 (NLT)

This is the beginning of the most famous passage in the Bible concerning spiritual warfare. I want to briefly explore the specific parts of the Christian's armor, but first let's take a quick look at this introductory statement that sets the tone for this vital discussion.

Have you ever heard someone say "I am my own worst enemy"? I have. But that is a false statement! God's Word teaches here that your true enemies are unseen, powerful, and all around you.

Also note that the order listed here is "rulers, authorities, powers, and forces." This same list appears other places in Scripture. What's being pointed out and discussed here is the fact that Christians are in a battle—an epic and life-changing struggle— for their very lives. It's like saying there are "generals, captains, sergeants, and privates" among the enemies you are up against.

As we will see in a moment, this is a prequel to a very vital list of specific list of equipment needed for this epic battle. But before I get to that, let's think about an interesting comparison from the world of modern sports.

For this example, I'll use the Dallas Cowboys and football, since players must gear up for the battle they face each week of the season.

Pretend you are on the team, and the game is scheduled for noon on Sunday. You and your teammates take your bag of gear (helmet, shoulder pads, cleated shoes, etc.) and congregate with your team on your side of the field around 11:45. Just before the noon kickoff, you and your teammates carry your equipment bags out onto your side of the field and sit down to have a picnic lunch. You notice referees gathering around the field as the stands fill, and you hear a loud whistle and see the other team rushing toward you as you enjoy your meal. As they attack, you and many of your comrades are injured. "Why do bad things happen to good people?" you scream above the noise of the crowd.

I contend that it's because you didn't suit up in your body armor for the battle you faced. Spiritually, that's what Christians are commanded to do each day, but few take it seriously.

Lord, please help me to remember that this is war, the enemy is unseen and very organized, and that I must gear up for the battle, or I am quite vulnerable. In Jesus's name, amen.

Unseen Kingdoms

"God created everything in the heavenly realms and on earth. He made the things we can see and the things we can't see—such as thrones, **kingdoms**, rulers, and authorities in the unseen world."

Colossians 1:16 (NLT)

Although I've never heard a sermon on this, the Bible teaches here that there are unseen rulers, authorities, kingdoms, and thrones. This implies territorial angelic or demonic authorities, depending on who these unseen rulers and authorities report to—God, or Satan.

Remember, in the unseen there are no "grey" angels. They are either on God's side, or they are on Satan's. We like to talk about how many things in our world today are "grey" areas, but I wonder if there is any doubt as to how God views the activities we love to call "grey."

Lord, I can't see the world of demons and angels—yet—but I know it's there. Help me to realize that every choice I make here in the seen realm each day either leads me closer to You or farther from You. Help me to make the right choices so often that they become a habit. In Jesus name, amen.

Power from God

"A final word: Be strong in the Lord and in his mighty **power**."

Ephesians 6:10 (NLT)

When you become a Christian, you are making an eternal covenant with God, the King of the universe. Your King; your covenant partner is reminding you that when you think you don't have the strength to carry on, you really do, since you have access to God's strength through your covenant relationship with Him.

You are now in His family, adopted, and co-heir with Christ: "So if you belong to Christ, you are now part of Abraham's family, and you will be given what God has promised" (CEV).

Before we leave that point, there's something else you need to know.

In the United States of America, adopted children can never be disowned—they will be a part of that family until they die. In fact, I have heard it said (though I don't pretend to be an expert; a lawyer would be needed to confirm this possibility) that some states even require that adopted children be included in the will. God is like that, too. Sure, you can turn your back on Him, but He will never turn His back on you. He will never write you out of His will. Rest in that fact.

> And remember, the blood of Jesus is what makes your covenant relationship possible: "My blood, which confirms the covenant between God and his people."
>
> Matthew 26:28 (NLT)

Lord, I literally can't make it today—or any day—without your strength. Thank You for the blood of Jesus, which confirms my covenant with You, giving me access to Your power and strength to make it through. Whenever Satan makes it look like there's no way through this, please remind me of that fact. In Jesus's name, amen.

No Partially Prepared Soldiers

Have you ever watched a war movie? Did you notice that every soldier is fully dressed for battle? None of them forgot their shoes, their helmet, their rifle, or their pants. They are prepared and focused. Should the Christian soldier be any different? Not according to God:

"Put on *all* of God's armor so that you will be able to stand firm against all strategies of the devil."

Ephesians 6:11 (NIV)

Partially prepared soldiers are really unprepared soldiers, vulnerable soldiers. Don't be partially prepared. Gear up, because a) Satan has many strategies—it's plural, and b) without your armor, you're quite vulnerable.

Lord, forgive me for being ignorant in days past of the strategies and tricks of Satan. Help me to be more prepared in the future than I have been in days past. Open my eyes to how he is working against me and how I can stand firm against all these strategies. In Jesus's name, amen.

Invisible Enemies

"For we are not fighting against flesh-and-blood enemies, but against evil rulers and authorities of the *unseen* world, against mighty powers in this dark world, and against evil spirits in the heavenly places."

Ephesians 6:12 (NLT)

You might think you're fighting against a flesh-and-blood enemy, but you're not. You are doing battle against evil forces who are visible in this four-dimensional world (length, width, depth, and time). You are fighting an unseen, powerful enemy: evil spirits living in a dimension where they can see us and work against us, but we can't yet see them. Keep that in mind.

Satan is not alone. Note here also that your unseen "enemies" are plural—as in more than one. I point that out, because I had someone tell me once when I was teaching that there was only one demon: Satan. This Bible verse teaches otherwise. You have multiple unseen enemies working in concert with each other to lead you far away from God in every possible way. They are organized.

Also notice that your enemies in the unseen realm are not just weak, pesky little problems; they are quite powerful. In fact, they are called "mighty" powers. But don't be discouraged, because "He that is in you is greater than he that is in the world" (1 John 4:4). Christians have the assurance of the Holy Spirit, once they have been baptized into Christ (Acts 2:38).

Lord, the evil powers against me have no power against You. They can't hold a candle to You. Thank You for the power I have through You, and right now, in Jesus Name, I claim that power so I can overcome those who stand against me. In Jesus's name, amen.

Guaranteed Survival

"For this reason, take up all the armor that God supplies. Then you will be able to take a stand during these evil days. Once you have overcome all obstacles, you will be *able* to stand your ground."

Ephesians 6:13 (GWT)

Putting on all the armor of God isn't just suggested; it's commanded—for your own protection. If you do this, God makes you a promise: you will be able to stand your ground against your enemies. Bank on it. But remember, your survival is dependent on your obedience in gearing up for the daily battle you face as a soldier for the King.

Lord, I realize that whether I live or die in this battle I will survive, since Jesus conquered death. Death holds no power over me anymore. And just as Your loyal servants in days past gave their all for You, I am willing to do that right now. Help me to stand firm on the ground You have put me in charge of. In Jesus's name, amen.

Belt of Truth

"So then, take your stand! Fasten *truth* around your waist like a belt."

Ephesians 6:14a (GWT)

Under the ancient covenant, covenant partners exchanged belts. The belt was where you hung your weapons. This symbolized an exchange of strength. Once you are in a covenant relationship with God, you have access to His strength, which is more than enough for any situation you face. Without God's strength there are times when you would be overwhelmed, but with His strength you can conquer anyone and anything. Rest in His strength, and wear it like a belt. God's truth is the source of that strength. Don't listen to the world. They want you to think that truth is relative, that there is no absolute truth. That's a lie. God's unchanging truths are recorded in His word. Read it. Know it. Use it to get you through today, because today is all you have.

Lord, I acknowledge that Your truths are at the heart of how I can stand firm where You have placed me. I also admit that I haven't been as grounded or focused on the truth as I should have been. Forgive me for this, grant me grace and courage to change that, and use me to uphold Your truths in every situation. In Jesus's name, amen.

Breastplate of Righteousness

"And having put on the breastplate of *righteousness*."

Ephesians 6:14b (ESV)

The breastplate protected the heart and vital organs. Don't go into battle unprotected or unkind. Wear God's righteousness in everything you do. Remember, you are an ambassador for the greatest kingdom in the universe—God's Kingdom.

33

Lord, forgive all the unrighteousness in my life. Open my eyes to anything in me that separates me from You. And Remind me that every day and in every decision I am representing the kingdom. In Jesus's name, amen.

Shoes of Peace

"And having shod your feet in preparation [to face the enemy with the firm-footed stability, the promptness, and the readiness produced by the good news] of the Gospel of *peace*."

Ephesians 6:15 (AMP)

This verse talks about putting on the "shoes of peace" in many versions, but I like the detailed, expanded version offered in the Amplified Version of the Bible:

First of all, this speaks of being prepared. Not only are most Christians completely unprepared today, they don't even have Bible study on their "to do" list. Without the "firm-footed stability" that knowing God's word provides, you are sure to fail. In addition, once Christians are confronted with a difficult situation, their lack of preparation for it (by spending time with God) makes their response, most often, inadequate at best, and dismal at worst. Anger often surfaces, since they don't know how to respond, or, worse yet, silence. When good people do nothing at all, evil will always prevail.

Lord, although the battle with Satan and his forces is a war, remind me that I am to bring peace in the seen world to every situation. I want to be full of grace and truth just as Jesus was. Grant me a soft voice and gentle spirit as I respond and react to the daily trials of life. In Jesus's name, amen.

Shield of Faith

"In addition to all of these, hold up the shield of *faith* to stop the fiery arrows of the devil."

Ephesians 6:16 (NLT)

We'll talk more later about how Satan uses fear because it pushes your faith out to make room, but for now let's notice that your faith shield protects you from all attacks—and you will be attacked. It's not a matter of "if," but "when."

> *Lord, I confess my faithlessness in so many past situations. Please forgive me and give me the courage to grow in this area. I know it's vital—it's the shield that protects me from demonic attack. Help me overcome all my fears and trust Your hand, Your words, Your provision. In Jesus's name, amen.*

Helmet of Salvation

"Accept God's *salvation* as your helmet."

Ephesians 6:17a (NCV)

The helmet protects the mind, the place where you make a decision to follow Christ and obey His commandments. Satan wants you to neglect to protect your mind so you'll be vulnerable to his tricks and strategies.

> *Lord, help me to be deaf to Satan and his forces, and tuned in to hear Your voice and Your messages to me every day. Use me to Your glory! What can I do for the kingdom today?...*

Sword of the Spirit

There is only one offensive weapon in your Christian armor: your Bible.

> "And take the sword of the Spirit, which is *the word of God.*"
>
> Ephesians 6:17b (NCV)

Note that this was the only defense Jesus used against Satan during His forty days of temptation in the desert. And even when Satan misapplied the truth, Jesus quoted the appropriate passage to counter the attack. You need to know God's word and use it when temptations come at you, too. God has no grandchildren, only children. Are you a child of God? Prove it by spending time with your Father.

> *Lord, please forgive me for neglecting Your instructions to me in the Bible. Give me a renewed daily commitment to Bible study and prayer. Help me do better in the future than I have in the past. Thank You for that forgiveness, and for Your patience with me as I work to change into someone more like Jesus. In Jesus's name, amen.*

Now What?

Now we come to the part I don't hear anyone talking about. Once you're dressed in your armor, what next? Let's look back at the Guidebook (the Bible):

> "*Pray* in the Spirit at all times and on every occasion."
>
> Ephesians 6:18a (NLT)

🔖

"Stay alert and be persistent in your *pray*ers for all believers everywhere."

Ephesians 6:18b (NLT)

❧

"And *pray* for me, too. Ask God to give me the right words so I can boldly explain God's mysterious plan that the Good News is for Jews and Gentiles alike."

Ephesians 6:19 (NLT)

Lord, what do you want me to learn from this? Have I misunderstood prayer? Often in the past I have used prayer as a last resort to my struggles. Does this teach me that prayer is what I need to be doing as I face every new obstacle?...

Prayer IS the Battle

Three times in the next two verses we are instructed to pray! Pray all the time (verse 18a). This goes along with the command in 1 Thessalonians 5:17: "Pray without ceasing." I pray all the time. I pray when I drive (with my eyes open), when I go to sleep, and when I wake up. I pray when I'm worried (don't you?), when I have a sick friend, and when my children have me concerned. Never stop praying. Once you're dressed for battle, hit your knees. That's truly where the real battle lies.

Lord, thank You for opening my eyes to where the true battle is. Please remind me of this until I learn to make it a habit in my daily life. Nudge me when I forget and try to solve my problems without Your input. In Jesus's name, amen.

Putting on the Armor Each Day

I have met folks who wake up every day and literally pray through these items of battle gear: the belt, breastplate, shoes, shield, helmet, and sword. They name each item in the battle suit and spiritually put it on, asking for wisdom in the battles they will face that day. That might sound silly to you, but the truth is that if you're not facing some tough situations in daily life, then you're probably not much of a force for Satan to recon with; you're probably not doing much for God's side.

I don't mean to sound harsh, just being truthful. Have I become your enemy because I tell you the truth? I hope not, because over and over in the scriptures God's followers are urged to know His truths and stand up for them as they serve Him each day.

Here's what that prayer might look like each morning:

Lord, thank You for the night's rest and another new day to serve You. Thank You for Your watchful care. Lord, I'm ready to dress for the day: help me to wear the belt of truth and never compromise; help me to wear righteousness as my breastplate wherever I go; help me to wear the shoes of peace when anger tries to rise up in me; show me where to direct my shield of faith as the attacks come; thank You for Salvation available through Jesus Christ—now help me to wear it as my helmet and protect my mind from unholy thoughts, concepts, and lies all around me today; and Lord, when I lay my head down on my pillow tonight, please help me to know Your truths better than I did when I woke up today. Now, Lord, what can I do for Your kingdom in Jesus Name today?

Why Did God Say, "Kill Them All"

"You must not worship the gods of these nations or serve them in any way or imitate their evil practices. Instead, you must **utterly destroy them** and smash their sacred pillars."

Exodus 23:24 (NLT)

I began to share this concept in Bible classes many years ago, pointing out that when they offered sacrifices to idols, demons were in the unseen accepting these blood sacrifices.

I was teaching this material in a Bible class one day, and one of the church leaders who had been a Christian for over forty years said "Steve, I don't know about that. What makes you think there are demons behind the idols?"

Honestly, I was a little surprised a man so knowledgeable of the Bible would question this, but here are the two verses I shared to answer his question. One is from the Old Testament, and one is from the New Testament.

> "They worshiped their idols, which led to their downfall. They even sacrificed their sons and their daughters to the demons. They shed innocent blood, the blood of their sons and daughters. By sacrificing them to the idols of Canaan."
>
> Psalms 106:36-38 (NLT)

> "Am I saying that food offered to idols has some significance, or that idols are real gods? No, not at all. I am saying that these sacrifices are offered to demons."
>
> 1 Corinthians 10:19-20 (NLT)

Although the Old Testament can be confusing to many people, it has much to teach us. Galatians 3:34 says it's a "schoolmaster" for us: "Wherefore the law was our schoolmaster to bring us unto Christ, that we might be justified by faith" (KJV).

One common assault on Christianity today attacks with this statement: "If there is a God and He wants the best for us, why did He tell the Israelites to kill every man, woman, and child in Canaan?" Good question, wouldn't you say? How would you answer it?

In order to understand why a loving God would command this, we need to know a little about the culture of idol worship that existed in that land. There were actually seven nations in the land of Canaan when God sent Israel to conquer them:

> "The Lord your God will bring you into the land that you are going to occupy, and he will drive many nations out of it. As you advance, he will drive out seven nations larger and more powerful than you: the Hittites, the Girgashites, the Amorites, the Canaanites, the Perizzites, the Hivites, and the Jebusites."
>
> Deuteronomy 7:1 (GNT)

Not only was it 7 to 1 against Israel, but there weren't that many Israelites to begin with. Each of these nations was larger and more powerful. Remember, the Israelites had just spent 430 years in slavery while these seven nations had been training for war and conquering. Big difference—sort of like David versus Goliath.

Lord, when the odds against me look unbeatable, remind me that with You on my side ... I can't lose! In Jesus's name, amen.

Temple Prostitutes

> "No Israelite man or woman must ever become a ***temple prostitute***."
>
> Deuteronomy 23:17 (NCV)

These nations (that God had instructed Israel to utterly destroy) worshipped many regional demon gods in unique ways. One of the unique "acts of worship" involved temple prostitutes.

Sometimes the "worshipper" would slip away from the idol on display to a small portico for sex acts. Other times the "worshippers" had group sex in front of the idol. Keep in mind that this was long before the development of antibiotics that help with "social diseases," so joining in their "worship services" or marrying into these nations meant that you would be infected with the diseases this sort of lifestyle leads to.

Now you know why God said to a) kill them all, and b) don't intermarry with them. Makes sense, doesn't it?

> *Lord, when the odds against my own success seem impossible, remind me that all things are possible for You. Also, remind me, Lord, that when Your instructions seem harsh, You always have a reason that has my best interest in mind. In Jesus's name, amen.*

Passing through the Fire

Now let's move on to the phrase, "he made his son pass through the fire."

> "There shall not be found among you anyone who **makes his son or his daughter pass through the fire**, or one who practices witchcraft, or a soothsayer, or one who interprets omens, or a sorcerer."
>
> Deuteronomy 18:10 (NKJV)

I never heard a sermon on this topic. It's not the sort of thing sermons usually cover, children in the audience and such. It's an ugly reality. An evil ceremony. A physical act with a supernatural hope. It's a desperate endeavor to get the favor of the "gods," and the One True God hates it. Here's how it works and what it's supposed to accomplish.

There was an iron (graven) image made to represent and honor a territorial demon god (like Molech or Chemosh). The image portrayed the god sitting and holding out its hands like to receive something. Many times in the frenzy associated with these demon gods in Canaan there was group sex or sex in a small adjacent room with a temple prostitute (male and female). Sexual acts were often done in the worship of this evil being.

Keep in mind, here, that at this point in history there was no penicillin or strong antibiotics that would help cure people from the sexually transmitted diseases that were commonly passed along through this bold and flagrant unrighteousness. Now you can begin to understand why God told His people not to inter-marry with these people. And not only would this mean deadly, incurable diseases, it would also introduce false gods into the nation of Israel.

The iron god was solid in the front, but hollow underneath, leaving room to build and stoke a big fire. At the height of the frenzy that included lewd sexual acts and drunkenness, the ded-icated worshippers who wanted the "gods" to favor them with good weather and bountiful crops would move forward toward those open arms of the iron deity and pitch their newborn infant (preferably sons, because they were much more valuable than daughters) into those white-hot demonic arms. The child would burn, melt, and die very quickly after coming in contact with the idol. If that doesn't sicken you, you've watched too many hor-ror movies and have lost your tender conscience that warns you about the evil around you.

Note also before leaving this verse in Deuteronomy 18 that God associates this evil activity with other great acts of evil like witchcraft, soothsayers, and sorcerers. All occult activity is for-bidden by God and harmful to humans.

Perhaps now you can begin to understand why God wanted them all dead: men, women, and children. The evil they spread was the especially bad variety.

Note finally that it's very similar to the modern-day evil of abortion—except that they killed the baby right after birth rather than right before. And it saddens me that as of the writing of this book the United States of America has aborted over 50 million babies. Some say these 50 million lives would have made a mas-sive positive economic impact by paying taxes, contributing to charities, and inventing solutions. Who knows how many geniuses and gifted leaders and inventors we have killed before they had the chance to make a difference. I have noticed that everyone who is pro-abortion is alive. Ironic, isn't it?

Lord, just like the prophet Daniel, I now confess the sins of my nation. Forgive us for calling little lives just blobs of tissue. Psalm 139 teaches us that even before we are born you know exactly how many days we will live and every single word we will say. And in the New Testament we learn that you even know the exact number of hairs on our heads—which is a constantly changing number, revealing an ongoing knowledge and love You have for us. Help us to see all those around us through Your eyes, and have compassion and love for them. In Jesus's name, amen.

"You saw me before I was born. Every day of my life was recorded in your book. Every moment was laid out before a single day had passed. How precious are your thoughts about me, O God. They cannot be numbered!"

Psalm 139:16-17 (NLT)

"And the very hairs on your head are all numbered. So don't be afraid; you are more valuable to God than a whole flock of sparrows."

Luke 12:7 (NLT)

What Was Paul's Thorn in the Flesh?

"I have received such wonderful revelations from God. So to keep me from becoming proud, ***I was given a thorn in my flesh***, a messenger from Satan to torment me and keep me from becoming proud."

2 Corinthians 12:7 (NLT)

❧

"I will reluctantly tell about visions and revelations from the Lord. I was caught up to the third heaven … I was caught up to paradise and heard things so astounding that they cannot be expressed in words, things no human is allowed to tell."

2 Corinthians 12:1-4

As Paul leads up to a discussion of his "thorn in the flesh," he reveals that he was allowed to enter and see the "third heaven," and that he saw "paradise." The sights and sounds there were so wonderful and astounding that our current language can't begin to express and communicate the beauty there, and, even if it could, he wasn't allowed to tell about it. Wow. It must have been absolutely awesome.

"That experience is worth boasting about, but I'm not going to do it."

2 Corinthians 12:5 (NLT)

What a privilege and honor! Paul got to see something that apparently no other human has seen. I thought it might have been the same place Ezekiel was "caught up" to see, but he actually was allowed to write about it in detail, so that must not have been the same place.

"I have received such wonderful revelations from God."

2 Corinthians 12:7a (NLT)

This wasn't the result of too much pizza, or an upset stomach—these revelations came directly from God, so God is the one who kept Paul from telling others about it. I have often wondered why this might be the case. Perhaps God loves you so much that He wants to see your face when He reveals it to you rather than letting you in on a few details through the inadequate avenue of language ahead of time. Just a thought.

> "Therefore, in order to keep me from becoming conceited,
> I was given a thorn in my flesh, a messenger of Satan, to
> torment me."
>
> 2 Corinthians 12:7b (NLT)

The Greek word used here for "messenger" is often translated "angel," so it could actually accurately read, "an angel of Satan." What is an angel of Satan? It's a demon. It's a fallen angel who followed Satan in his rebellion against God, and is a part of the spiritual forces of evil in the unseen at work against you (Ephesians 6).

What was the true purpose of Paul's thorn in the flesh? It was to keep him from becoming conceited. Pride and conceit go together. What was it about these revelations that would nurture a response in Paul like that? I suppose it was knowing that he was allowed to see—in the flesh—what no other human being was ever allowed to see: not Abraham, not Moses, not David, not Joseph—not nobody! So whatever this thorn in the flesh was, I believe it was just as unique and drastic (from a human standpoint) as the revelations he had been allowed to see, somehow humbling Paul continually and helping keep him focused on his earthly goal.

If I had seen a scene like that (the third heaven) I don't think I'd ever forget it. I might visualize it every time I got a little discouraged. And, more than that, I would probably be greatly tempted to use that argument against Jewish and Roman opposition when they tried to attack my ministry and work for the kingdom of God. Wouldn't you? Perhaps, just perhaps, Paul was tempted in that same way, and that "messenger of Satan" (demon) would remind him of that, though unseen and unknown by all others in Paul's presence!

"Three times I pleaded with the Lord to take it away from me. But he said to me, 'My grace is sufficient for you, for my power is made perfect in weakness.'"

2 Corinthians 12:8-9 (NLT)

Daniel prayed to God for twenty-one days in Daniel 10 before God's messenger arrived to answer. Why did God cut Paul off, say no so quickly, and even instruct Paul to stop asking for that—after only three prayers on this topic? Because the revelations were too great; they needed to be offset. When you see something that wonderful and beautiful, it stays with you, and you need help for the rest of your life to keep that in perspective. And, apparently, the only thing that would work in this case was a permanent, ugly, rebellious, smelly demon that went with Paul wherever he went. I bet he wasn't happy with that assignment, don't you? Just sayin'…

> *Lord, deliver me from evil. Protect me for the tricks and strategies of the devil and his angels. Guard me against the principalities, authorities, and evil spirits in the unseen realm. Grant me discernment in this important matter, and lead me far away from temptation. In Jesus's name, amen.*

Grandma Was a Witch

"You must never sacrifice your sons or daughters by burning them alive, practice black magic, be a fortuneteller, **witch**, or sorcerer."

Deuteronomy 18:10 (GWT)

I once spoke in chapel at a Christian High School on the topic of spiritual warfare. I told the story of the atheist who walked into Burger King on a Saturday morning and began a conversation with me because I had an open Bible in front of me. (I tell the whole story at the end of *My Search for the Real Heaven*.)

After chapel ended, a tall young man rushed up to me in the confusion of the two hundred high schoolers leaving t'.e gym and said to me "I need to talk to you today."

"Okay," I said, "I'll be here all day, and I'm having lunch in the school cafeteria. Want to catch me in there and talk?"

"Yes," he replied, "see you then."

I spotted him walking toward me in the cafeteria a little after noon. He was easy to see—tall, good looking, and obviously coordinated, probably a star on the basketball team there. His eyes caught mine, and it was evident he wanted me to slip away from the group and talk privately.

He was calm and confident. The story he was about to relate was so bazar and supernatural. It didn't fit with the calmness he exhibited in walk.

I had finished eating, so I threw away the disposable plate and utensils and spotted an empty table. I nodded him in that direction. As we sat, he had a very serious expression, the expression of a man much older than he was, his eyes focused and intense on me as he told me his story.

"My grandmother was a witch," he started.

I don't know about you, but I had never had a conversation with anyone that began like that, especially not a young man only in high school. He was sixteen. He continued.

"When I was born, she somehow got some of my blood and offered it to a demon. I can see them."

I guess that if I had never realized that Paul's thorn in the flesh was demonic (and that perhaps he was the only one who could see the demon assigned to torment him), I might not have believed this young man. But I confess that he had my attention.

He calmly and methodically related his life story over the next few minutes, along with his father's family connections to the demonic. It was shocking. Unless you believe what the Bible says about angels and demons, you would think you were hearing scenes from a horror movie. A really "good" one.

47

His parents were divorced, but apparently, his mother had no help or encouragement from her family and was forced to rely on her ex-mother-in-law for baby-sitting help from time to time; a common story for single moms. You see it every day, that's for sure. Then this young man told me about the final straw, the event that severed their relationship with the witch for good. Here's what happened.

It was another one of those instances when his mom was in a bind and forced to ask Grandma Witch to baby sit. He made it sound like Grandma was probably very deeply involved in the occult, with regular episodes of potions, incantations, and satanic rituals. And apparently Mom finished her errands quickly, arriving home before expected. All he could remember was his mom bursting through the front door while he was sitting in the middle of the floor chanting some phrase over and over. He couldn't remember the words, but he did remember his evil grandmother getting more of his own blood and urging him to repeat those same words over and over and over. Sick stuff.

That was it for his mother. She threw this awful woman out of their living room and out of their lives forever. They even moved far away from there to be sure the woman didn't sneak in uninvited. This evil has found them more than once. Each time, they just move far away—again.

Lord, deliver me from evil. Please. In Jesus's name, amen.

Fear vs. Faith

"It was by *faith* that Moses left the land of Egypt, not *fear*ing the king's anger. He kept right on going because he kept his eyes on the one who is invisible."

Hebrews 11:27 (NLT)

Have you ever woken up in the middle of the night thinking about some serious problem? I have. And I think it's fairly common. It might be a serious problem at work.

You lie there and think, *What can I do to fix this? If I don't find a solution soon, this will cause another serious issue. If that happens, then it's all going to get much worse. If things get much worse, there's no way I can handle it. If I can't handle this, I'll have to give up. If I give up, people will lose respect for me. If that happens, I'll bring shame on my family and on the church. Wouldn't I just be better off dead? Wouldn't my family and my church be better off if I simply died before all these bad things can happen?*

Maybe you don't take it that far, but that's exactly how it starts. And if you let it, these fears get worse and worse until—by morning light—the problems are way too big for anyone to handle, let alone you.

It's a lie. It's all a lie from Satan. It's designed to steal your soul, but if he can't convince you to take it that far, it's designed to rob your effectiveness. This includes your effectiveness as a father, as a husband, as a Christian businessman, and especially as a leader in your church.

But the good news is this: you have a choice as to whether or not you let this happen. Literally.

You can choose what to focus on, and it's really quite simple. You get to choose between fear and faith.

> *Lord, help me realize that I have a choice of what to focus and meditate on: fear or faith. I've tried fear; I've let my mind wander down many paths of various fears. It didn't help anything. Now I'm ready to try faith; ready to focus on all Your promises instead. From here on, every time fear starts to grip me, help me to choose the path of faith. In Jesus's name, amen.*

Choosing Fear

"Jesus responded, 'Why are you *afraid*? You have so little faith!' Then he got up and rebuked the wind and waves, and suddenly there was a great calm."

Matthew 8:26 (NLT)

If you let yourself focus on your fears, something terrible—even sinister—begins to happen. They grow bigger and badder (please excuse the slang). Seriously. The more you think about them, the more your mind enlarges their badness, their scope, and their eventual repercussions. They literally grow into monsters.

If this sequence happens in the night when you wake up, by morning they are enormous. Way bigger than you'll ever be able to handle. They especially grow in the dark. Why? Satan likes to work at night.

The good news is that the real life result of the problems you lay there and worry about at night never end up as bad as you imagine they will. That's how Satan works. He amplifies your fears until there's no room at all for faith.

However, if you make a different choice, those same fears evaporate.

Let me tell you a little secret about Satan: he does his best work in the dark.

Lord, when I wake up in the dark and start to worry, help me to know who to pray for. Give me the name of someone who's in trouble and needs Your help desperately. And may this process keep me from focusing on my fears. I lay all my fears at Your feet and trust You with the outcome. In Jesus's name, amen.

Choosing Faith

*"**Choose** today whom you will serve."*

Joshua 24:15 (NLT)

Faith is a choice. It's a real, literal, daily one. And if you're willing to make that choice, fear disappears like the morning dew. But it takes training. You must train yourself to focus on your faith in God's promises.

> "Seek ye first the kingdom of God, and his righteousness; and all these things shall be added unto you."
>
> Matthew 6:33 (KJV)

If we really seek the things of God above all else, He promises to provide all of your other needs. Not 10 percent, not 50 percent—all. You either believe it, or you don't.

> "God causes everything to work together for the good of those who love God and are called according to his purpose for them."
>
> Romans 8:28 (NLT)

Do you love God? Are you actively seeking your kingdom purpose? Then everything that happens to you is allowed by God, or is the will of God. Do you really believe this? If you doubt this Scripture when you face difficulties in life, then you really don't believe what God says in Romans 8:28. It's a faith issue, a trust issue.

Consider what Joseph said to his brothers—the very ones who sold him into slavery:

> "You intended to harm me, but God intended it all for good. He brought me to this position so I could save the lives of many people."
>
> Genesis 50:20 (NLT)

51

Meditate on what Moses says here in Deuteronomy to Israel about the fact that God let many bad things happen to them:

> "Remember how the Lord your God led you through the wilderness for these forty years, humbling you and testing you to prove your character, and to find out whether or not you would obey his commands. Yes, he humbled you by letting you go hungry and then feeding you with manna, a food previously unknown to you and your ancestors. He did it to teach you that people do not live by bread alone; rather, we live by every word that comes from the mouth of the Lord. For all these forty years your clothes didn't wear out, and your feet didn't blister or swell. Think about it: Just as a parent disciplines a child, the Lord your God disciplines you for your own good."
>
> Deuteronomy 8:2-5 (NLT)

Zechariah even goes so far as to say that the fires and trials of life lead to a dependency on God:

> "I will bring that group through the fire and make them pure. I will refine them like silver and purify them like gold. They will call on my name, and I will answer them. I will say, 'These are my people,' and they will say, 'The Lord is our God.'"
>
> Zechariah 13:9 (NLT)

David even says that his own suffering taught him a most valuable lesson:

> "My suffering was good for me, for it taught me to pay attention to your decrees."
>
> Psalms 119:71 (NLT)

These are all promises from God, the same One who spoke the earth into existence. The mighty King of the universe, which literally means, "everything that exists everywhere."

He promises protection (Genesis 15:1), provision (Hebrews 3:18-19), personal involvement (Matthew 28:20), and in the end, purification for all His people (Titus 2:14).

The real question is this: Do you believe Him? It's that simple.

You get to make the choice. Do you believe the lies Satan is constantly throwing at you (especially in the dark), or do you believe the Creator? Whom do you trust? And this is the most important and difficult decision you'll ever make. Here's why:

Fear and Faith are Mutually Exclusive

Fear and faith cannot coexist. As it turns out, if you let yourself focus on your fears, your faith evaporates, but if you train yourself to focus on your faith, your fears melt away like snow in the sunshine.

Have you ever thought about it? It's impossible to be full of faith and fear at the same moment! We like to try to mix them like we mix hot and cold water, but that just comes out in a Christian's walk as a lukewarm life. And we all know how God hates that (see Revelation 3:14-19 and the discussion of how God feels about the lukewarm church in Laodicea). He will just spit you out and be rid of you.

So begin today to train yourself. Trust God's many promises. Read them. Study them. Meditate on them until they become an integral part of your daily life and activities. That way, you begin to learn to recognize when Satan's throwing new lies at you, and you'll also know why he's doing it: he does it to destroy your faith and separate you from God forever. Don't let him.

Lord, throughout my whole life my reaction to problems has been fear. Then on that backdrop of fear I have tried to work out all my own problems. From now on, help my natural reaction to become prayer and trust in Your provision. You have already brought me through so much—so I have no reason to believe You won't get me through this, too. Open my eyes to the path I should take. May it be the one that brings you the most glory. In Jesus's name, amen.

One Possible Solution

"But be sure to *fear the Lord and faithfully serve him.* Think of all the wonderful things he has done for you."

1 Samuel 12:24 (NLT)

Try the following. It works for me.

One day it dawned on me—maybe God is waking me up to pray for someone else. I'm His servant, aren't I? I pledged my life to Him and His agenda at my baptism, didn't I? Perhaps someone else needs me right now to pray for them.

So one night I said to the Master, "Okay, Lord, I'm awake. Is there someone You want me to pray for right now?" Often, the name of someone I know would pop into my head. I would pray for them, and then go back to sleep. Soundly.

Finally, remember that you aren't the only one dealing with this issue—David had the same problem: "I prayed to the LORD, and he answered me, freeing me from all my fears" (Psalm 34:4, NLT)

Lord, I am Your servant; it's not the other way around. You aren't my "Santa in the sky," available to do my bidding or fix each problem as I go down my list. Help me to be willing to change my plans and my schedule to best suit Your work around me. Lord, most of my life I have decided what I wanted to do for You and the Kingdom and then asked you to bless it. Now I realize how arrogant that is. Open my eyes to where You are already at work, Lord, and show me how to join in. In Jesus's name, amen.

Daniel 10—A Peek into the Unseen World

"Don't be afraid, Daniel. Since the first day you began to pray for understanding and to humble yourself before your God, your request has been heard in heaven. I have come in answer to *your prayer*. But *for twenty-one days* the spirit prince of the kingdom of Persia blocked my way."

Daniel 10:12-13 (NLT)

It's easy to read through this chapter quickly and miss what's really going on here. The first few times I did that—that's exactly what happened—I missed it. But one day a few phrases caught my eye, and I referred to some commentaries. It made for some very interesting reading, and based on their "enlightened" opinions, I looked closer, prayed for open eyes to see the truth here, and it came to life in my mind. I hope these thoughts bless your life.

The bottom line is that if you really want a cool peek into things that happen in the unseen realm, spend some time in Daniel chapter 10. Let that chapter bounce around in your noggin awhile, and you'll be shocked to learn what it reveals. It's like pulling a curtain back on a world humans don't usually get to see. And out of sight, out of mind, right? But here, we're talking about truth, and the truth is that there's a whole other realm nearby, just out of sight with principalities, powers, and authorities. This chapter reveals some incredible insights about some of them and how this whole realm interacts.

It starts out rather blandly, with Daniel in "mourning" and probably fasting from his normal diet and bathing schedule for three whole weeks (verse 2 and 3), but then you learn later in the chapter that it was actually three whole weeks focused on prayer (verse 12 and 13).

Next thing you know, Daniel is down by the river and sees a frightening, blood-curling, terrifying vision. Scripture doesn't really indicate exactly what the vision shows him, but several phrases about Daniel's response to it indicate that it must have been awesomely scary.

I have thought a lot about that, and another verse that comes to mind is the passage where Elisha and his servant are surrounded by the enemy of Israel, the King of Aram, in 2 Kings 6:15-16. When Elisha's servant is terrified one morning as they discover they are surrounded by their enemy, Elisha simply prays that God will open the servant's eyes. He is suddenly able to see an angelic army surrounding the human army. His fear is gone. Those who were with them were greater than those who were with King Aram.

In this case, the angels are focused on the enemies of Israel, and there is no battle going on.

In Daniel's case, however, this angel messenger is in the middle of a battle between angels loyal to God and demonic entities (led, apparently, by the prince of Persia, a local authority). This battle is going on in the unseen for 21 days, Daniel is continuing to pray for answers from God and this angel is trying to bring them, but this evil, demonic spirit prince stationed right there in Persia—where Daniel is living—is blocking the way; keeping God's message from getting through. Michael (possibly with additional troops) arrives to help with the contest so the angel charged with the message for Daniel can get to him.

I don't think it's too much of a stretch to consider this possibility: the spirit prince of Persia was near Daniel, though unseen, right there in Persia (thus being called the "spirit prince of Persia") keeping God's angelic warrior from his task. This goes on for twenty-one days (angels probably don't need sleep on a daily basis like humans do), and they are doing battle the entire time until Michael shows up with some reinforcements. Then the messenger angel is able to simply step past the battle and get to Daniel. Then Daniel (like Elisha's servant) is given the ability to see into the invisible realm, and he faints immediately because of the awesome battle he gets a glimpse of. If you saw one of these invisible wars in your current body, it would probably overwhelm you, too. It's just a thought. Regardless, the sight made Daniel faint and fall face down onto the ground.

Let's look at it in detail:

There was a "man" in white linen (at least he looked like a man, verse 5).

He had a belt made of pure gold on his waist (verse 5).

His body looked like precious metal (verse 6). Wish mine did.

His face flashed like lightning (verse 6).

His eyes were like flaming torches (verse 6).

His arms and legs looked like polished bronze (verse 6—guess he had a good tan).

His voice was overwhelmingly loud and mighty, like the voice of a multitude of men came out of one man's mouth (verse 6).

Daniel faints. He heard the voice, saw the mighty angel (and perhaps the battle in the background that even included Michael, an archangel with high authority), and his body can't take it. He literally blacks out.

The angel messenger was powerfully strong, and he lifted Daniel up after he fainted (verse 9-10). And remember, Daniel is no meek weakling. We're talking about the same guy who said, "Bring on the lions—I've got God. No problem." Right?

When he told Daniel to get up in his powerful voice, he told him first that he was special and precious to God. I don't know about you, but in a moment like that, I think I'd enjoy hearing that, wouldn't you?

"Steve, God thinks the world of you!" I like the sound of that. Lots of days I really need to hear that; don't you? But to actually hear that personal message from the King of kings—that's something.

Then he tells Daniel to listen carefully. He helped Daniel to stand, but he was still so shaken up by what he saw that he just stood there trembling—probably more focused on this than on God's message.

Fear makes people tremble. When fear overpowers a human mind, the connected body just shakes. Have you ever tried to concentrate on something when your body is shaking? Impossible. The angel knows this, so he issues a command that goes to the root of the real issue (the fear) and says, "Don't be afraid."

Then he basically tells Daniel that he's been trying to get there for three weeks, the local opposing principality, the local spirit prince of Persia, was stopping him. And it appears that this local spirit prince was equal in power to this messenger angel, because he apparently could have stopped this message from getting through indefinitely. But Daniel's persistent prayer brought an important angelic reinforcement: Michael, an archangel.

This encouragement from the angel helped Daniel recover some, but he still wasn't himself, so the angel touched him.

Amazingly, the touch gave Daniel new strength, and he began to feel normal again. Also, the encouraging words form this God-messenger also made him stronger. He improved enough to pay attention and was finally ready to hear God's message. "Speak to me," Daniel finally said (verse 20). He was ready.

The angel then gave Daniel his itinerary! He said that after he finished delivering Daniel's message, he had to return to the fight, presumably relieving Michael, so he could go back to wherever he had come from. He also knew that the battle with the spirit prince of Persia would ultimately end, and that there would be another battle after that with a different spirit prince: the prince of Greece.

At that time, Persia ruled the known world. Guess who eventually conquered the Persians. The Greeks (verse 21)! So this angel knew at least some things about the future and the enemies he would face.

> "Truly I tell you, whatever you bind on earth will be bound in heaven, and whatever you loose on earth will be loosed in heaven."
>
> Matthew 18:18 (NIV)

Lord, help me to know exactly how to pray. I now realize that when I pray in the seen, things are happening in the unseen. As as child of the King, my words have power.

Keep Praying

> "For **you answer our prayers**. All of us must come to you."
>
> Psalm 65:2 (NLT)

Many preachers who I have heard during the course of my life have said, "God answers prayers in three ways: 1. Yes, 2. No, and 3. Not now, maybe later."

This chapter in Daniel reveals a fourth possibility: The answer is on its way, being delayed by evil forces. (So keep praying.)

Lord, help me to be persistent with my prayers until you fulfill the request, or, as you did Paul, until you tell me to stop asking for that thing. In Jesus's name, amen.

Excuses are Often Lies

> "Moses pleaded with the Lord, "O Lord, **I'm not very good with words**. I never have been, and I'm not now, even though you have spoken to me. I get tongue-tied, and my words get tangled."
>
> Exodus 4:10 (NLT)

Have you ever noticed that excuses are often lies?

When my boys were young, they helped me learn that. "He hit me back," one would say.

"Who started it?" I often asked. Fingers pointed in every direction.

As all parents know, this list could go on and on, a never-ending cycle, like a merry-go-round that never lets anyone off.

The Truth about Moses

"Moses was taught all the wisdom of the Egyptians, and he was *powerful in* both *speech* and action."

Acts 7:22 (NLT)

What excuses are you telling God and others? Are they true, really accurate? Evaluate your reasons for not leading a prayer, teaching a Bible class, speaking up for Jesus at the office. And remember, one day you'll have to repeat those same excuses to God. Then ask yourself: "What will He say about that?"

"Tell me again why you never took a spiritual leadership roll in your family?"

"Why, again, did you vote for this candidate? For economic reasons?"

"What was is in my Word that made you think church attendance was unimportant?

"Who made you think social drinking would never have any consequences?"

Satan wants you to decline all kingdom projects. Satan wants you to put your own kingdom above God's—in every way possible.

God, however, wants you to be willing to change your schedule for His. He wants you to put His agenda over your own. He wants you to wake up to the fact that He is the Master and you are the servant.

Lord, just like Moses, I have made excuses for why I wasn't putting Your kingdom and Your agenda first in my life. Forgive me. And help me to change that from now on. Give me strength and courage to do what's best instead of what's most comfortable. In Jesus's name, amen.

Trading Enemies

"You have come to Jesus, the one who mediates the **new covenant** between God and people."

Hebrews 12:24 (NLT)

God has always worked by covenant. There are seven covenants in the Bible, and symbols are associated with every one. Blood is always involved. We now live under the new covenant, which is mediated by Jesus Christ, God's Son.

I covered all the details of the ten steps of the ancient covenant in *My Search for the Real Heaven,* but I do want to focus on one of these ten steps for the purpose of this book, and especially this chapter about our enemy.

Make no mistake, Satan and his forces are your enemy. They are to kill, deceive, steal, and destroy (John 10:10). But why? If Satan is rebelling against God, why is he focused on us?

The answer lies in a little-known discussion about covenants. Let me explain.

One of the steps in the ancient covenant was the exchange of weapons. I give you my sword, and you give me yours. This symbolizes the exchange of enemies. Who was God's enemy? Satan. So he became ours:

"Stay alert! Watch out for *your great enemy, the devil*. He prowls around like a roaring lion, looking for someone to devour."

1 Peter 5:8 (NLT)

Who was our enemy (because of our sin)? Death. So Jesus came and conquered death.

> "But thank God! He gives us *victory over sin and death* through our Lord Jesus Christ."
>
> 1 Corinthians 15:57 (NLT)

Resurrection isn't just for Jesus. It's the future of every Christian (who dies before the second coming).

Another aspect of the covenant involves exchanging strength. We can't defeat Satan with our own power, but we have God's strength to defeat Satan because of the covenant.

Christians often have a "grasshopper" mentality when they ought to have a "giant" mentality. We feel like grasshoppers of goodness in a world filled with evil and ugliness. It's overwhelming at times. It generally makes us feel helpless and hopeless and useless because the big bad world is getting bigger and badder and uglier by the day.

While I admit it's easy to fall into that sort of thought pattern—especially by watching the evening news—keep in mind that David, a man after God's own heart, focused on God instead of the giant in front of him. The story of Goliath is a perfect example.

Remember what David said when he discovered Goliath taunting Israel each day:

> "David asked the men standing near him, ... Who is this *uncircumcised Philistine* that he should defy the armies of the living God?"
>
> 1 Samuel 17:26 (NIV)

∾

"Your servant has killed both the lion and the bear; this *uncircumcised Philistine* will be like one of them, because he has defied the armies of the living God."

1 Samuel 17:36 (NIV)

What did that mean? What does circumcision have to do with anything?

It had everything to do with it! Circumcision was the mark of the covenant between God and His people, a physical connection symbolizing the bond between the two. (Just like baptism is for the Christian today.)

Another aspect of a covenant relationship was that when your covenant partner was attacked, you were obligated by contract to go help. Their enemy is your enemy. So when God's people were attacked, the covenant meant He would come help. So here is what David was really saying:

"Who is this uncircumcised Philistine? Who is this guy taunting us? He isn't in covenant with the one true living God! He is no match for God! We are in covenant with God! I don't care if he's twenty feet tall—he's no match for someone in covenant with God! I'll take him on in God's name because I *am* in covenant with God."

That's why David wasn't afraid—he knew for sure that God was on his side!

By the way, do you know why he wanted five stones? Because Goliath had four brothers!

The story is summarized in 2 Samuel. The father of Goliath was a giant who had five sons, and they all fought for the Philistines. Goliath was killed by David himself, and his four brothers were ultimately killed in combat with David's men (2 Samuel 21:22). The only one of the four who was mentioned by name in Scripture was Lahmi (2 Chronicles 20:5).

Goliath was apparently the first of the five to die because the others are mentioned later. David figured one stone per giant. Now that's confidence—in God!

> *Lord, thank You for the peace that comes from knowing that death isn't the end. Thank You for demonstrating my own future resurrection by resurrecting Jesus Christ. Forgive me for fearing death, and remind me that death no longer holds power over me because of Jesus. Also, Lord, when Satan attacks and the circumstances appear to be overwhelming, remind me that I have access to Your strength to endure and overcome—because I am in covenant with You. In Jesus's name, amen.*

Visit to a Psychic Medium

"Saul then said to his advisers, "Find a woman who is a **medium**, so I can go and ask her what to do."

1 Samuel 28:7 (NLT)

After my book, *My Search for the Real Heaven*, became a little more widely known, I began to get invited to speak at many churches around the country—and many different kinds of churches. It was a great honor. One of these churches was in a small town in North Arkansas. This particular congregation had two services and a total Sunday attendance of around four hundred. First they invited me to come lead a weekend men's retreat. There were around eighty men in attendance. They were so excited about my message and style that they invited me back for a spiritual warfare series for the whole congregation and an outreach, using my heaven study to draw visitors from the surrounding community.

I taught the Sunday morning combined Bible class and led both worship services. I focused that day on prayers that Satan hates and gaining a better understanding of spiritual warfare. It was lots of fun for me and was well received by all. They had been planning the outreach for several weeks, so this is what I told them in closing that Sunday:

> "You have all invited your neighbors and friends for the outreach that begins tomorrow night and runs through Thursday evening. Before you go to bed tonight, I want you to say a very specific prayer: '*Lord, I have invited my neighbor to come to this outreach on heaven. Please help them to come. In Jesus's name, amen.*'"

Now I don't know about your church, but most churches have a tough time getting 20 percent of their members to attend anything on Monday night. They had 50 percent! Literally two hundred of their members came to the civic center (a great neutral location that's usually more likely to be successful getting visitors to come). There were also two hundred community visitors who attended! We averaged almost four hundred a night, and the last night it was pouring down rain!

It wasn't me (nobody knew who I was; I'm a "nobody"—but God still uses "nobodies" like me). What was it? Prayer still works, and God is still on the throne.

I always invite questions at the end of each session, and this generally leads to lively interaction and interesting perspectives. Three of the most common questions I always get on heaven are:

1. Are there animals in heaven?

2. Is it a sin to be cremated?

3. Will we have our memories in heaven and recognize folks we knew in this life?

It's always fun to see what questions people have, but some aren't comfortable asking their questions in front of a big crowd, so we also announced each evening that if they had a question they preferred to ask in a more personal setting that I would be available to discuss it at breakfast or lunch the next day. Each evening they announced where I would have breakfast and lunch. I had every meal with five to twenty-five people!

At one of these meals, Bob told me this story about his wife's family.

Bob's wife, Phyllis, was not raised in a Christian home. She became a Christian after meeting Bob. Phyllis had a sister who had never become a Christian. Their mother got Alzheimer's disease when she was in her late sixties and had to be put in a care center. Before getting Alzheimer's, the sisters were aware that their mother had hidden a large amount of money somewhere in her home. After getting this disease, she obviously couldn't remember where she had hidden the money. Phyllis's sister made an appointment with a medium, and demanded Phyllis accompany her to the appointment. Being a Christian, Phyllis didn't want to go, but her sister insisted, so she finally agreed.

At first, Phyllis wasn't impressed. The things she "knew" from communicating with "spirits" on the other side weren't unusual or unique. But then she "seemed" to know some details about the death of a loved one who had died in war. Finally, the subject of the hidden money came up. Phyllis's sister asked the medium point blank where it was. After a moment of hesitation during the exchange of information between the medium and the "other side," the medium answered the question in an abrupt and straightforward manner, revealing exactly where the hidden loot was located. They returned to the house and found the money in the exact location the medium had indicated.

You see, it isn't that Satan and his evil forces don't have power; it's that it's the wrong kind of power. It's power focused on leading people away from God instead of toward Him. What greater weapon than money? Satan loves it when we focus on money!

> "For the love of *money* is the root of all kinds of evil. And some people, craving money, have wandered from the true faith and pierced themselves with many sorrows."
>
> 1 Timothy 6:10 (NLT)

Lord, stop me from being too focused on money. I have to pay my bills and take care of the needs of my family, but don't l·t me become obsessed with it. Help me to see it simply as a tool that helps me accomplish my Kingdom work for You—nothing more. In Jesus's name, amen.

The Day a Demon Spoke to Me

"Then Jesus said ... The *demon* has left your daughter."

Mark 7:29 (NCV)

I will never forget that day. I was in high school and could have been driving that old truck because I had just gotten my driver's license—a prized possession to any teenage boy. This meant I could go out on an actual date with a girl or visit a friend who lived far away—my ticket to freedom.

It was summer in Central Texas, and it was hot. We were busy with one of our many projects, as Dad always had a list ready when the summer break began. This one involved hauling old rock. The rocks came from an old, broken-down fence, one the early settlers in Mason County had laboriously constructed. It had been replaced by a modern barbed-wire fence, complete with t-posts down the middle and braced cedar corner posts strategically placed at the corners and other points where the land rose or fell with the hill country terrain.

We had filled that old pickup with all the old shocks could handle—and a little more. Dad wasn't one to waste space, energy, or fuel. We made the most of every minute and every trip. My little brother and I had elected to ride in the back, sitting on top of the rocks, enjoying the breeze as we rocketed down the old dirt road from the rancher's property at the blazing speed of about thirty miles per hour. One of life's simple pleasures that many today will never enjoy because of seatbelt laws and careful parents. It was a safer time to live and grow up, and a safe little town to live in.

We finally left the dirt road and pulled onto the pavement, and Dad gunned it. Now we were going at least forty-five or fifty, and you could hear and feel the shocks groan with each pebble in the highway. Dad slowly increased his speed until we were going about fifty-five. For some reason I leaned over the tailgate and stared at the pavement. It felt like we were going one hundred, though I knew that old truck could never go that fast, especially with a load that heavy. It was hypnotic, almost like I was falling into a trance, a feeling I had never experienced before.

That's when it happened. The voice. I heard it. I know it sounds crazy, and I can tell you for a fact that it felt crazy, too, but that voice still haunts me because of what it said, and I wonder how different my life would be if I had obeyed that voice.

I know now that it was the voice of Satan or one of his demons, but at the time I didn't really make that connection. It was specific. It was direct. It was apparently assigned to me. And I'm really glad I didn't obey that voice. But I confess to you that I almost did. Almost.

What did it say? It was simple, just one word. One single word that I almost obeyed. Almost, but not quite. If I had obeyed it, the whole course of my life would have changed. I'm so glad I didn't obey.

It said, "Jump."

Lord, help me to be deaf to all the words of Satan and his forces and very tuned in to all Your words and communications. In Jesus's name, amen.

"Then *the devil* took him to Jerusalem, to the highest point of the Temple, and *said*, "If you are the Son of God, *jump* off!"

Luke 4:9 (NLT)

Strongholds

"We use God's mighty weapons, not worldly weapons, to knock down the *strongholds* of human reasoning and to destroy false arguments."

2 Corinthians 10:4 (NLT)

There are many strongholds in the world around us, giving Satan a foothold in our lives. We need a beachhead-like Normandy, some small piece of territory where we can make a stand and begin to fight the surrounding evil.

We need to remember first of all that we currently live in enemy territory. We must acknowledge there is an enemy before we begin to fight against him, right? Satan is currently in control, the god of this world (for now).

"Satan, who is the *god of this world*, has blinded the minds of those who don't believe. They are unable to see the glorious light of the Good News. They don't understand this message about the glory of Christ, who is the exact likeness of God."

2 Corinthians 4:4 (NLT)

How do we fight? What do we do to prepare? How did Jesus fight Satan when He was tempted for forty days? He quoted the Scriptures:

"Then he said, 'You son of the devil, full of every sort of deceit and fraud, and *enemy* of all that is good! Will you never stop perverting the true ways of the Lord?'"

Acts 13:10 (NLT)

Do you know the Scriptures? It's never too late to begin to study and learn them. Well, I guess that's not really true. You can wait until it's too late, but I hope you don't. I hope you'll begin now, before it is too late.

"But the truly happy people are those who *carefully study God's perfect law* that makes people free, and they *continue to study it*. They do not forget what they heard, but they obey what God's teaching says. Those who do this will be made happy."

James 1:25 (NCV)

Okay, how else do we fight? We talked about it in chapter 1: Pray.

Study and pray. That's the way. Start right away. Don't let Satan stay in control of your life.

"For though we live in the world, we do not wage war as the world does. The weapons we fight with are not the weapons of the world. On the contrary, they have divine power to demolish strongholds. *We demolish arguments* and every pretension that sets itself up *against the knowledge of God, and we take captive every thought* to make it obedient to Christ."

2 Corinthians 10:3-5 (NIV)

Lord, please help me first to recognize the footholds that Satan has in my life; especially those that have become his strongholds. Next help me to renounce them, reject them completely, and then defeat them daily in my life—from now on. In Jesus's name, amen.

Fishing for People

"Jesus called out to them, "Come, follow me, and *I will show you how to fish for people!*""

Mark 1:17 (NLT)

Is there someone in your life you want to lead to Christ? Is there someone who's hurting, lost, or lonely? Have you exhausted all your options in the past, accidentally burned your bridge to them, or said something that makes you think there's no hope for you to reach them?

Most of us think this way about at least one person in our lives. We feel like we've messed up so royally that there's no way they would listen to us, no way we can turn them around, no way they will ever find Jesus and peace—at least not through you. But that's a lie from Satan. Truth be known, you are probably still the biggest threat in their life to Satan's control over them. So don't give up.

> *Lord, right now I'm thinking about _____. You know how close to them I've been for a long time, and You know how much they need You in their life. I've tried to make a difference, but I'm worried that I've messed up in the worst possible way; worried that I've ruined my witness with them. Remind me, Lord, that they know I'm human; that I make mistakes. Touch their heart, Lord, and show them my love for them. Don't let me give up. Rebuild anything I've accidentally torn down. Repair any holes I've put in our relationship. And please give me the right words at the exactly right moment to still make a difference in their life—an eternal difference. In Jesus's name, amen.*

Demon List

"Those from Babylon worshiped idols of their god *Succoth-benoth*. Those from Cuthah worshiped their god *Nergal*. And those from Hamath worshiped *Ashima*. The Avvites worshiped their gods *Nibhaz* and *Tartak*. And the people from Sepharvaim even burned their own children as sacrifices to their gods *Adrammelech* and *Anammelech*."

2 Kings 17:30-31 (NLT)

In the first part of this chapter, there is a list of some demons called by name in the Bible. I was teaching this in a Bible class one day when one man raised his hand and said, "Steve, how do you know those are demons?" You may have the same question, so I'll offer that answer here and now for you, too.

Although both these passages were mentioned earlier, they bear repeating in this context. First, let me offer an Old Testament passage that confirms this:

> "They worshiped their idols, which led to their downfall. ***They even sacrificed their sons and their daughters to the demons.*** They shed innocent blood, the blood of their sons and daughters. ***By sacrificing them to the idols of Canaan.***"
>
> Psalm 106:36-38 (NLT)

This New Testament verse help confirm this idea:

> "Am I saying that food offered to idols has some significance, or that idols are real gods? No, not at all. I am saying that these ***sacrifices are offered to demons.***"
>
> 1 Corinthians 10:19-20 (NLT)

As hard as it may be to swallow, these Bible passages point out that when humans sacrificed their children to idols, demons were present—though unseen—accepting these blood sacrifices. (This makes me wonder what occurs and who is present in the many medical facilities where abortions are performed in the United States—all 55 million-plus of them so far.)

> *Lord, forgive us for just seeing abortion as a removal of unwanted tissue. Help us to see these events through Your eyes. Help us to have compassion and loving respond to all those affected while still standing up for the truth—that it's murder. In Jesus's name, amen.*

Zazoos

"And I remind you of the ***angels who did not stay within the limits of authority God gave them*** but left the place where they belonged. God has kept them securely chained in prisons of darkness, waiting for the great day of judgment."

Jude 1:6 (NLT)

I believe there's actually a Bible name for the "angels who did not stay within the limits of authority God gave them." They are called "demons." And although the demons mentioned here did something so heinous that they are locked up, waiting for judgment, many demons are free to serve Satan's purposes in our daily lives, working to lead us away from the pathway to heaven. C.S. Lewis was one of the premier proponents of this thought process, and his study of this resulted in a best-selling book that caused him to land on the cover of *Time Magazine* in 1947: *The Screwtape Letters*.

If you believe demons were only a first-century phenomenon designed to help the early church survive and thrive, I invite you to reread Ephesians 6, or chapter 1 in this book. They are many. They are focused. They are powerful. And they have strategies, implying great intelligence.

As I was compiling and completing the list of demons actually named in Scripture, I was sitting at a long red light on highway 80 in Longview one day near Popeye's Fried Chicken. I glanced over at "Zazoos," a long-time establishment that had offered palm reading and tarot card revelations for many years in that same location. I thought about the name. I repeated it out loud several times. Then, without really thinking, I said out loud, "Lord, that name sounds like some of the strange names in the Bible of demons. If that is a demon that runs that place, I pray You would bankrupt them. In Jesus's name, amen."

Though it had been right there in that ugly, old, faded-brick building for over twenty-five years, when I passed by that spot a couple of weeks later, I was completely shocked—it was bankrupt. "Out of business," and "For Rent" hung in the windows.

What am I trying to say? Am I saying that my prayers are more powerful than others? Am I saying that if you really want something accomplished you should ask me to pray for you? No. I'm probably just the only one who thought to pray about it. Prayer is powerful. Prayer works. All Christians are children of the King. The King spoke the world into existence—His words have great power. But since Christians are His kids, we have power, too. Remember, "what you bind on earth will be bound in heaven," and "what you loose on earth will be loosed in heaven," or in the "heavenly realms."

God wants to do more in your life, all around you. He's anxiously waiting for you to approach Him and ask for it. And He's ready to drop whatever He's doing and listen to your requests.

For those of you who have difficulty with that, let me offer this simple story to illustrate the relationship.

I was president of my company for twenty-eight years. I was very busy and had important meetings and planning sessions all the time with different department heads. But if my son called, I was to be interrupted. Always. No matter how busy I was, I always had time for my boys. They were more important than anything. They were why I worked; they gave my life purpose and meaning and joy, and they knew it. You need to realize that same thing about your heavenly Father. He's ready to drop everything He's doing just for you. Talk to Him—often.

Lord, thank You for adopting me into Your family through Jesus. Remind me that You want a closer and closer relationship with me; that You think of me as Your own natural-born son—just like Jesus. In Jesus's name, amen.

Suicide Down the Street

"The Lord said to him, 'What are you doing here, Elijah?' Elijah replied, "I have zealously served the Lord God Almighty. But the people of Israel have broken their covenant with you, torn down your altars, and killed every one of your prophets. *I am the only one left, and now they are trying to kill me, too.*"

1 Kings 19:9-10 (NLT)

Depression. It can descend on anyone. Elijah was committed to God, serving Him daily, and in grave danger. The danger was real. His coworkers were all being killed for their work, and he knew he was walking around with a target on his back. It was only a matter of time.

Then God arrives and says, "What's happ'nin'?"

"What's happ'nin'?" Elijah replied. "I'll tell you what's happ'nin'. I've been workin' my buns off for you, and all my coworkers are dead. Everybody's turning to demon worship, and our lives as prophets for You are over. Done. Finished. In fact, I'm the only one left, so they're all looking for me to finish the job. That's what's happ'nin'."

Ever felt that way? I have.

"Lord, I've been faithful, and you let this happen. How could you? Why? What good will this do?"

I've been there. I've done that. It hurts. It feels like the skies are brass and my prayers can't go up even though my mouth is still moving. I'm sure Job felt that way. Many have. Probably every single person who has started a business and then it looked like they would fail. It's a lonely feeling. You feel responsible— even if you know it isn't your fault. You're going to suffer, right? So it must be your fault. You start to review every decision you made and question your abilities. We've all done it at one time or another. Self-doubt. It's one of Satan's most powerful tools.

Self-doubt can lead to self-blame. Self-blame makes you review in your mind how every around you is going to suffer because of your mistakes. Sometimes there are people around you pointing that out—true or not. So where does it lead?

Ultimately—if you let it—it leads you to think this thought: *If I just die, then everyone around me will be better off.*

It's a lie, but Satan can make it sound so true.

That's what happened to a boy around the corner from me. He was a senior at Pine Tree High School. He was active and well liked. He had numerous friends, and he participated in many school activities. Everything looked fine on the outside. His parents had no clue—no clue that he was terribly upset on the inside. He was blaming himself for some of what we would call minor problems. I don't really remember what it was, but it came out later. It may have been a tiff with a girl, a bad test grade that was about to be posted, or an issue with a friend. It doesn't matter now, does it?

Or maybe it does. Maybe we should review what it was so we—who are still living—can get the proper perspective about our own issues. Bad grades can get better with focus. Relationships will change with time. Pain will lessen as we focus on new activities.

But for this young man—it's over. His problems seemed bigger than any possible solution, and he was convinced it would be better if he were dead (that's how Satan works). So he shot himself in the head in his own bedroom.

Now that I'm in ministry, sometimes I get asked about suicide: "Does everyone who commits suicide go to hell?" How would you answer that? It's a tough question, isn't it? Especially in light of the fact that some religious groups have that as a fact, even offering relatives a chance to "buy" their way out of hell into heaven.

I've thought about it a lot, and I'm sure I don't have all the answers for these hurting families. I've prayed with some, hugged them, cried with them. Only God can judge, but here's what I finally decided after my study of spiritual warfare:

Suicides are caused by people who are deceived. They are deceived into thinking that everyone around them would be better off if they were gone, simply out of the picture. They are ignoring all the activities associated with their actual death. Things like the blood, the gore, the shock of the people who find them, the emptiness felt by all who love them, the funeral, the publicity, and many other factors. They are tuned in only to the voice in their head that assures this is best, even preferable by all concerned.

Still, it's deception. And all of us are deceived in one way or another. My deception may not lead me to commit suicide, but I'm still deeply deceived in some other aspect of my life. In light of that, I don't think personally that suicide is a guaranteed one-way ticket to hell. In addition, we must balance this with the possibility of a chemical disorder or another tangible medical reason.

When I interact with people who are dealing with this sensitive issue, I pray with them, hold them, and tell them what I just told you. No need to sugarcoat the truth, and we can't know right now for sure. But I certainly don't think that every person who ever committed suicide is in hell. Just sayin'.

Remember, David was depressed after his realization of the public nature of his sin with Bathsheba (Psalm 51).

> *Lord, I pray for a special blessing on all those who have lost a loved one to suicide. Heal their pain. Grant them peace. Put people around them who can encourage them and speak kind words to sooth their soul. In Jesus's name, amen.*

Praying for God to Help Me Put This Book Together

"As for God, His way is perfect; **the word of the Lord** is tried. He **is a Shield** to all those who trust and take refuge in Him."

2 Samuel 22:31 (AMP)

In 1998 I got to go to Israel with a big group. (I am a tightwad and discovered a cheap deal by going with a group of 450. It was great!) I learned a lot about the Jews there, which makes the Bible much more interesting to me. Jewish homes put a mezuzah on the door of their homes. The word actually means, "doorpost," but it's basically a small parchment of Scripture that is rolled up

77

and put in a small, decorative case. It's visible, but now obvious, like God is there, but not "in your face." The parchment itself is called the Shema, but the device altogether is usually referred to as the mezuzah.

They take Deuteronomy 6:4-6, and 9 literally, where God commands them to write His laws on the door frames of their houses and on their gates. We might think it's silly now, but remember, this same God sent fire from heaven on Nadab and Abihu when they didn't get the fire from exactly where God had specified!

Although hanging a mezuzah is generally thought by Jews to be a simple act of obedience, as in "God said to do it, so we did," it's also a symbol of their commitment to God's word, and the constant reminder that God's word protects. That's what all those promises are all about, right? Eternal life, a home with God, and a resurrection are a few that come to mind. And it's literally true, God's word does protect. Trust and obey, for there's no other way, right?

Every time a Jew leaves his home or returns to it, they kiss the mezuzah or touch it. Or they touch their lips with their fingers and then touch their fingers to the mezuzah, a transferred kiss, sort of like blowing a kiss to a departing loved one.

I thought about that—a lot. God's word protects. Then and now. Forever, right? The thought bounced around in my pea-sized brain and kept on bouncing, like a Superball that just keeps on going and going and going. God's word protects. They touched it every time they passed it. It protected them. It protected their home. God's word was all about protection from the true enemy: Satan and his demonic forces.

Then I got invited to speak to a group of counselors at Bible camp. They deal with hurting children every summer and work to demonstrate God in their lives in every way possible. Many of these kids come from difficult homes and cause various problems for the counselors. So I got creative. I love to do wood work and I had some four-by-four oak beams stacked and dried. I took one of these that was about four-feet long and cut one end into a sharp point. I took it to the camp and showed it to the counselors, a fine Christian group of college-aged teens, and gave it a name: "This will be your 'Prayer Stake' this summer," I said. I want each of you to sign it with this marker. They all signed it and placed it in the woods nearby. "When you have a problem child, just go to this prayer stake and pray for that child. Claim the child for God and ask for wisdom in dealing with him or her."

They did. I think they converted and baptized more kids that summer than they ever had before. Prayer still works, and God is still on the throne.

> *Lord, I need your protection for my home and my family just like the Jews did. Satan is still here; the enemy is unseen and active, trying to hurt, kill, and destroy. Please protect my home and my family. Help this house to be an environment free and clear from the deceptions and schemes of the enemy and all his forces. Use us to Your glory. In Jesus's name, amen.*

Larry Called

"You **guide me** with your counsel, leading me to a glorious destiny."

Psalm 73:24 (NLT)

Note: real names aren't being used.

I had been praying about how to put this book together. I didn't just want a write a book to make money (though I do have bills); I wanted to write a book to make a difference. Then Larry called, and as I look back on it now, I can clearly see it as an answer to that prayer.

"Steve," Larry said, "I need help with a friend who thinks he has demonic activity going on in his life. I have been trying to lead him to Christ for years, and God may be using this to do just that. Can you help me with him? Can I come over and give you the background?"

"Absolutely," I said, and he came right over.

> *Lord, please give me wisdom and discernment as I listen to Larry's story and choose how best to help lead Bill to Christ. Open my eyes to the best pathway. Use me in this situation to Your glory; speak through me; give me the right words at the right moment for Bill—words that truly make a difference. In Jesus's name, amen.*

Background on Bill

"Then **on the seventh day the child died**."

2 Samuel 12:18 (NLT)

Bill and Larry had been friends for many years. They each had a son about the same age, and had even been on hunting trips together. These four had a great time on one weekend trip to Llano, TX, and Hugh, Bill's son, killed a ten-point buck. Bill had gotten a virus and had stayed at camp to sleep off the illness, so Larry took the picture of the proud young man with his prize kill. It turned out to be the last picture ever taken of Hugh.

Hugh was smart, fun, and very active in his church. He taught Bible classes, went on trips with the youth group, and had chosen a Christian college to attend. He was a sophomore and very popular among the students.

Just a few days after the successful hunt to Central Texas, Hugh went over to his grandparent's home, close to his own, and offered to clean out the gutters. Leaves and pine straw were packed, and Hugh was just that sort of a kind, thoughtful person, offering to help his grandparents.

In a freak accident, Hugh fell off the ladder and hit his head on the concrete sidewalk. He went into a coma.

Although his Christian classmates had an around-the-clock prayer chain going for Hugh for days, the monitors showed absolutely no brain activity, and they finally had to take him off life support. It was Christmas Eve when Hugh died, and Bill and Carol were devastated. Bill blamed God and wanted nothing to do with religion.

Hugh had checked the organ donor box on his driver's license, so his heart saved one person, his lungs another, and so on.

Bill lived in rebellion to God. "Why would God let this happen to such a fine, religious young man with his whole life in front of him? Why would a loving God do that?" Many have asked the same question over the years and centuries. It's difficult for those close to the victim.

Larry continued with details about Bill. Bill's business was failing. His employees had betrayed him—friends of his whom he had given a job to and some he had trained. The economy had taken a downturn; they couldn't pay the bills, and some of his employees were going together in a business similar to Bill's while they were supposed to be working for Bill. They had hurt Bill in every way possible—personally and professionally. The office environment became filled with bitterness and greed. Betrayal is a bitter pill to swallow.

If all that wasn't bad enough, Bill now had to find a renter for the building, and there were some serious problems with it.

"What sort of problem?" I asked.

"Strange problems," Larry replied. "First of all, there were electrical problems—quite unique ones. Once, for example, several computers had the main boards fried at the same time with what appeared to be a power surge, but the electric company had put a monitor on the facility, and it wasn't a surge or a storm. This happened in spite of the fact that Bill had put surge protectors on the power lines coming into the building and also on every computer. It couldn't be explained. Also there were plumbing problems, bad smells apparently coming from nowhere, and they couldn't be rectified. Bill even went so far as to have all of the toilets replaced with new ones, but that solved nothing. There was a barrage of weird issues like this."

Larry continued, "Then there was a really strange thing. I'm not sure how to tell you this—not sure you'll believe it. Honestly, I'm not sure I believe it. But Bill is terrified from what happened last Friday night."

Now you need to understand Bill to appreciate this part. Bill is no wimp. He's no milk-toast, meek little sissy man who gets scared at the drop of a hat. He's big and tough. He's confident and had always been successful and bold—until now. He's stout, with big strong arms and lots of body strength. I wouldn't want to face him alone in a dark alley, to say the least.

"Okay," I replied. "What happened Friday night?"

"Well," he began, "it was after dark, and Bill and his wife, Carol, had gone out to eat. Then they stopped by the building to pick up some boxes. He had to empty the building and get it ready to rent. Carol was loading boxes in the truck. Bill was opening the door from the inside by pushing a button to release the magnetic lock. When he pushed the button, 'something' laughed in his right ear. He froze. He closed the door and pushed the button again to see if that is what made the sound. It wasn't. Bill said he would never forget what the menacing voice said."

"What was it?" I asked.

"Well," replied Bill, "It was a ferocious laugh right in my ear, like it was trying to say, 'I won, you lost.'"

Bill said this made him jerk his head around—looking for an assailant. There was no one to be found! He ran out to the truck where Carol was calmly sitting and waiting and jerked open the door. "Did you see anyone?" he asked?

"No," Carol said.

"Did you hear anyone?"

"No," she said again, and then she added, "What's wrong with you? You look like you've seen a ghost!"

Bill said at this point he was terrified, so he got in his truck with Carol, and said, "We're getting out of here."

"He's usually tough and strong, Steve," Larry said, "not scared of anything. But he won't go back to that property by himself again—unless it was in broad daylight. Will you go with me and talk to him tomorrow morning?"

"Absolutely, Brother. What time?"

Larry picked me up at ten that next morning, and we headed out for an appointment with Bill—and destiny. We were armed with prayers at the ready, Bible verses, a five-pound sledge hammer, and four thick angle-iron stakes about ten inches long. We were headed for quite a ride. What we were about to do was something I'd never heard of, but I felt God wanted us to do just that.

> *Lord, help everyone who suffers from the loss of a child. There may be no greater pain than this. Comfort them and give them peace in the middle of that storm. Put the right people around them—people who can offer encouragement and hope. And please open our eyes to the real battle that's going on all around us every day in the unseen. In Jesus's name, amen.*

Meeting Bill

"The effective, fervent *prayer of a righteous man* avails much."

James 5:16 (NKJV)

It was cold and windy that Saturday morning. Larry and I pulled up into the Brookshire's Grocery Story parking lot to meet Bill. It was only a block from their building with all the weird problems, but Bill wasn't about to go there by himself—not even in broad daylight.

Bill got out of his big diesel truck and got in the back seat of Larry's car so we could talk there a few minutes. That's where I met Bill. We exchanged names and shook hands, and I'll never forget the first thing he said to me.

Bill held his fingers close together, like you do when you're measuring a tiny amount and communicating it to someone else. "I'm this close to suicide," he said.

"Don't do that, Bill," I said. "We're going to pray together and help you through this."

Have you ever felt that way? Has your world ever seemed so hopeless that you at least thought those words? Satan is really good at getting us to blow things out of proportion in our mind, isn't he?

I want you to know right now that that Bill did not commit suicide. The things we did over the next few minutes to help Bill changed his whole perspective. Completely.

Lord, when I'm confronted with a situation I've never experienced before; especially if someone is hurting and thinking about doing something drastic, help me to have the right words to keep them from ruining their life. Give me words of hope and encouragement for them. In Jesus's name, amen.

The Property

"Go and **walk through the land in every direction, for I am giving it to you.**"

Genesis 13:17 (NLT)

I rode with Bill in his big Ford diesel the one-block trip to the tainted property while Larry followed us. I really don't know what else to call it—especially since what we did changed it so drastically.

The brown-bricked building sat on a relatively flat corner lot with pavement surrounding it. The back sloped gently upward. I got out and said, "Oh my goodness."

"What?" Bill asked as he got out his side and slammed the big, heavy truck door.

"Look around," I said.

Bill's head circled like an owl on a post. "What do you mean?" he questioned.

"This property is business poison." I replied. Almost everything it touched was out of business. Behind it was an out-of-business nursing home on a nice, grassy knoll. Clockwise to the right was an abandoned used-car lot. Three more office spaces across the street had "Office for Rent" signs in the front windows.

The only active business in the entire area —and this was the main highway going through a town of about 5,000—was an auto parts store, and it was obviously struggling. Saturday morning is when all the shade-tree mechanics are buying all their parts and working on their trucks, and there was only one car in attendance. Obviously, it was the man running the cash register. "I know the man who owns that chain," I told him. "He is in my small group at church and comes to my house every Sunday evening for our studies. He has thirty-two stores, and I can guarantee you that this one isn't doing so hot. The other thirty-one are probably carrying it, don't you think?" He nodded. "Just wait here a minute," I said.

With that, I was off. I left Bill and Larry there in front of the building while I walked the perimeter with a quick prayer on my lips. I hadn't planned it that way—it was just a spontaneous decision. It was almost like I felt an evil presence, and this was the only logical response: quick, focused prayer.

It took several minutes—it was a large lot. The side street bordered one side, the old folks home in the back, the auto parts store on the other side, and the four-lane highway on the front that was overshadowed by the abandoned buildings across the street, all standing there like silent guards casting their shadows toward the property in question. I silently asked God all the way around for wisdom, discernment, and for anything evil to be removed in the name of Jesus Christ and by His authority—not mine.

I was so focused on my petitions that I didn't know Larry and Bill were watching me all the way. When I had almost returned to the starting point in the front, Bill came over quickly, almost running. "What did you just do?" he urgently asked. "Something just changed—I felt it. What did you do?"

"Not much," I answered. I was just praying and walking.

With a serious look on his face Bill stared and said, "The prayer of a righteous man…" He knew the verse. It shocked me. Obviously he had some religious training in his background, or he wouldn't have known that verse. He had learned it and even memorized it at some point in his past. It gave me insight into his personality that I didn't have before. I filed it away.

Lord, many people have be raised to love You and know Your word, but have drifted away from that instruction. Use me to remind them that leaving you behind always means leaving life behind; it means death is all that's ahead. Wake them up to their true destination before it's too late. Please. Whatever it takes. In Jesus's name, amen.

Forgive First–Before They Ask

"Father, *forgive* them, for they don't know what they are doing."

Luke 23:34 (NLT)

I stood there facing Bill, processing the fact that he had committed at least one verse from the Bible to memory. He stood there standing back, and suddenly I knew what I had to say next. It was almost like I was watching a movie, like watching myself say what had to be said next. Larry had said that some of his employees had betrayed Bill, and Bill was about to stake this land for God, and I knew it wouldn't work unless Bill set his bitterness aside. So I told him.

"Bill," I began, "we're about to stake out this land and claim it for God, commanding in Jesus's name that anything evil here must leave. You are going to drive the stakes."

"Okay," Bill replied.

"But before you start, there's one thing you need to do."

"What is it?" he asked.

"All these people who have betrayed you," I explained, "you have to forgive them."

Bill frowned quickly, dropping his head to the left.

"Look at me in the eyes," I demanded. And Bill met my gaze with serious eyes.

"Bill, if you don't forgive them, it's like slitting your own wrist and expecting the other guy to bleed to death. It ain't gonna happen."

He didn't blink. He stared at me hard. I felt my heart beat in my ears. Who was I to tell him what to do? But it happened before I could even think; I spoke before I could even stop myself.

Finally Bill responded, "I understand. I'll work on that." His eyes were set and the frown had straightened into a line, like he had suddenly realized this important thought at truth that could keep him from his goal: peace.

I nodded. "Okay. Good enough," I replied. "Let's start," I instructed as I walked toward the nearer corner.

> "*If you don't forgive* other people, then *your Father in heaven will not forgive you*r sins."
>
> Mark 11:26 (NCV)

Lord, thank you for giving me the right instructions to help others find the freedom and peace they so desperately seek. I pray that many others will heed this advice. In Jesus's name, amen.

The Four Stakes

"They did not *conquer the land* with their swords; it was not their own strong arm that gave them victory. It was your right hand and strong arm and the blinding light from your face that helped them, for you loved them."

Psalm 44:3 (NLT)

After reviewing this forgiveness/bitterness issue with Bill, I felt we were ready to do what we had come for.

I told Larry about the big wooden "Prayer Stake" used at summer camp and suggested we make four metal stakes, write a verse on them, and claim the property to God; sort of like establishing a beachhead to work from like they did in WWII at Normandy. This is war, right? God's word protects, right? Okay. So let's put God's name on the line—I figure He was big enough to handle it. Don't you? Larry had cut some thick angle iron into ten-inch pieces and fashioned one end into a sharp point like an arrow or spear. These stakes were very heavy, very strong, not likely to bend.

The three of us walked toward the first corner, a grassy knoll with a city stop sign on the hump in the middle. Without even thinking, I said, "Bill, the first corner will be the hardest." Actually, I don't even know why I said it; it came out of my mouth before I could even process the thought, like my mouth was operating on autopilot by my brain. I had studied the Scriptures that had led to this plan, and it was as if my subconscious was now controlling my thoughts and words before I could think through it again, like a man who had researched for years on a topic and now his reflexes were taking over as he began putting his theory into practice.

Bill glanced at me out of the corner of his eye. I think he was wondering why I said that. Secretly I was, too.

Now you need to get this picture. Bill is a pretty big guy with muscular, powerful arms. He had obviously worked hard during his lifetime. It's just a small grassy knoll. It's a sledge hammer. What could go wrong, right?

I watched Bill as he knelt on one knee, focused on placing the iron stake with his left hand, and then began tapping it with the hammer in his right. *No problem,* I thought. He got it in far enough to get it to stand on it's own, and then started hitting it harder and harder. It went down slightly with each blow, but after it was about halfway in, there was a problem. Bill sensed it too and put his other knee on the ground. Now this big, tough guy was two-fisting the sledge, down on both knees, and putting the full force of his weight into every blow. It still wasn't cooperating.

I don't know if you've ever hit a thick piece of angle iron with a sledgehammer when it's obviously lodged against a boulder beneath the surface of the ground, but it makes a unique sound. And the force of a powerful blow does something unique to the end of the stake: it begins to spread. Every hit makes the steel spread out a little. The metal is too tough and short to actually bend, but with each pound and ear-shattering ring at the point of impact, the metal was compressing and the iron edge was getting a fraction wider.

As Bill continued, I panicked. I thought, *Oh no, I have put God's name on the line, and he's hit a rock. What am I going to do?*

Before I realized it, I had gently put my hand on Bill's shoulder and said, "You're doing great, Bill. Let me help you finish."

He was hitting it so hard that the nearby stop sign was trembling with each blow.

He looked up at me like I was crazy, and I knew exactly what he was thinking. He was twice my size and strength. If he couldn't get it in—I certainly couldn't. But he stood up and handed me the sledge with a small smirk on his face that said, "Give it a try if you like, but we're going to have to move it to another spot. There's no way it's going in all the way right here.

As I dropped to my knees and cocked the hammer I prayed silently for help. *Lord, I've put your name on the line in front of this unbeliever. You are big enough to handle this—and he is watching. Help me. In Jesus's name, amen.*"

I did have to hit it pretty hard, and it did take several blows, but I got it down level with the ground and then sunk it two or three inches. Then I stood up and headed toward the next corner like it was no problem at all, like I did this all the time and it was to be expected, and like it was especially normal for the first corner to be the hardest one. Inside, I was relieved and shocked.

I walked without looking at them in the face, partly because of the shock, and partly because I was focused on getting this thing done. Behind me I heard Bill say, "How did you do that? I was hitting it way harder than you."

"Don't worry about that," I responded without thinking. "It's a spiritual thing." They followed me like obedient puppies. Bill was probably shaking his head, and Larry was probably smiling. "The next one will be easier," I instructed—again without forethought.

It was a big lot, a lot deeper than it was wide. We walked in silence, Larry carrying the remaining three stakes, Bill holding the sledge that I had handed back to him.

The next spot certainly should have been easier—much easier. It was out in a grassy yard that covered the area sloping up to an abandoned nursing home that no longer met the state regulations for such facilities.

"Right here." I pointed. Bill obediently knelt and placed the second stake. The process repeated itself to the letter, except that this time it went about three-quarters of the way in. So much, however, was sticking out that a mower would definitely have hit it the next time it was mowed. Bill was on his knees, the piercing hit with each blow, and the metal edge getting wider with each release.

Again I spoke up, "Let me help you, Bill. You are doing great, but I'll have to finish this one for you, too."

Dumbfounded that history was repeating itself because of the extra effort Bill seemed to be putting out, he rose and handed me the mallet for a second time.

I descended with a little more confidence this time, thinking, *God got me through the first one without embarrassment. He can do it again.* This time it was easier. With only a few quick blows, and without even drawing back half as far as Bill (because I was afraid I would miss), I sunk the top of the metal several inches below the surface of the dirt beneath the thick grass. No mower would ever hit it now.

Again I got up and heard admiring desperation in Bill's voice, "How are you doing this? I am hitting it much harder than you are."

And again, before I could think, I responded, "Don't worry about it, Bill. You'll get the next one."

He did. He struggled a little, but we were half finished, and this third stake went in deep and pretty fast.

"Good job, Bill," I told him as we walked toward the fourth and final spot. "This last one will be the easiest."

He briefly gave me that "how-do-you-know" look. But when we got to the spot, I wished I hadn't said that. It was on the highway, and there was no grassy knoll to be found—just solid asphalt. In fact, asphalt ran to that corner solid from both sides, Bill's place, and the auto parts store next door.

I admit that my faith wavered a little at that moment. And I wished there had been some sort of grassy area. But Bill looked up more assured than ever. He confidently positioned the stake with his left hand in the general area and pounded away. It went in very easily. And, although he wasn't really surprised, he cocked his head and asked me what was on his heart: "How did you know that would be the easiest one?"

"I don't know. I just did. I can't explain it."

"Now we're ready to go inside and pray," I instructed as I walked toward the front door. They followed obediently.

As Bill was turning the key in the front door (the same door where he had heard the awful voice), I asked my next question: "Which room did you have the most weird things happen in?"

"Right back there in the conference room," he said as he pointed.

"Okay," I replied, "let's go."

The plan was for all three of us to pray, but Bill had told Larry that he really didn't know how to pray. Maybe he was just too nervous in light of his experiences in that building, but whatever the cause was, Bill needed a track to run on. Larry had written out a prayer for Bill to read—basically it was the sinner's prayer confessing Jesus as Lord and asking for His help and protection. Larry pulled out the paper with the prayer he had prepared for Bill and asked him to read it over, making sure he was okay with what it said. Bill quietly read the words and nodded that he was ready to go.

We turned on the conference room lights and sat around the end of the table holding hands. At this point the building just felt like an abandoned office, and Bill didn't seem at all upset to be inside—but glad, I'm sure, that we were with him.

"Tell you what," I said. "Let's let Larry start, Bill can go next, and I'll end that prayer. Is that okay?"

Everyone agreed as we bowed our heads, closed our eyes, and held each other's sweaty hands.

Larry lead a great prayer with words focused on protection, healing, and hope for a brighter future for Bill. Bill read his little sinner's prayer. Then I finished it up, asking for God to clean up that spot and use it as a starting point to bring hope and healing to the whole city. I ended with "In Jesus's name, amen" and looked up at Bill. There was something important he needed to understand.

"Bill, there's a story in the Bible about getting rid of a demon, but then that demon went and found seven other bigger, badder demons and brought them back to his former abode to live with him there. The person was worse off than they had been before" (Matthew 12:43-45).

"Bill, you are clean right now," I continued. Bill smiled and nodded like I had simply stated an obvious fact that no one would ever disagree with.

"But there's a problem: you're vulnerable. Acts 2:38 teaches that when you accept Jesus and are baptized, you receive the Holy Spirit. This is the protection you need against the enemies you face. I just want you to know that I am going to be praying that you will be baptized—to supplement your commitment to Jesus in a way that finalizes and announces your willingness to covenant with God from now on.

"You must repent of your sins and turn to God, and be baptized in the name of Jesus Christ for the forgiveness of your sins. *Then you will receive the gift of the Holy Spirit*" (Acts 2:38, NLT).

He looked at me with a very serious expression. "I understand," he responded. I nodded. Good enough.

The three of us ate lunch together, and Bill wanted to pay—in spite of his dire financial condition. I gave him a copy of my book, *My Search for the Real Heaven*, and Larry had helped him get a Bible—which he was now beginning to read.

We parted, and I went home feeling good about what we had done. Bill was a changed man—just from our short time together. He seemed more upbeat, and the wrinkles on his forehead seemed to have vanished.

The next day was Sunday, and I was singing in our praise team at church, so I sat near the front. We had a "meet-and-greet time" where we all stood for a few minutes to visit with friends and offer a kind welcome to all the guests. As I scanned the auditorium, I saw Bill smiling, almost running to the front to greet me.

"How are you?" I asked.

"Great, now!" he responded. "I've been reading my Bible. I've been reading your book on heaven. I slept all night last night— the first time in months!" His face was beaming, and there was no fear at all in his face. It was a very different man from the one I met the day before when he told me he was about ready to commit suicide.

Prayer changes lives. Prayer changes everything.

The very next Sunday, my prayer was answered. Bill and Carol responded to the invitation of Jesus Christ, came forward at the end of the worship service to publicly acknowledge Him, and were both baptized—by Larry. I videoed the historic event on my iPhone. God is Good.

The man who was ready to commit suicide the day I met him is now a committed Christian who sends me a Bible verse every day to encourage me. He also prays for me every day. He brought me a word from the Lord once. He goes on mission trips; he helped with the Tuscalusa, Alabama tornado cleanup. He has been to areas hit by tornados to help those who are hurting. He is living for God, praise His name.

Lord, thank you for sending Bill into my life. Thank you for blessing him through me. I pray that the witness of his story will help enlarge Your Kingdom all over the world. In Jesus's name, amen.

Another Suicide Story

"Saul groaned to his armor bearer, 'Take your sword and kill me before these pagan Philistines come to taunt and torture me.' But his armor bearer was afraid and would not do it. So *Saul took his own sword and fell on it.*"

1 Chronicles 10:4 (NLT)

I told this story to a preacher friend from Arkansas, and he sort of got quiet. He asked several detailed questions but seemed detached somehow. A few months later he called, and I found out why.

"Hi, Steve, this is Jack. [Not his real name.] Do you remember telling me the story about the stakes and the guy you converted as a result of it?" he asked.

"Sure," I replied.

"Well," he continued, "that story struck a chord with me. We had recently purchased a new home and moved our family across town. It was a nice neighborhood and a bigger place. But a few months afterward, my son told me about some thoughts he was having about suicide and some cravings he was feeling toward some types of Internet pornography. Your story made me think I should stake out our new home—just in case.

"So I did. I went to Home Depot and bought four angle-iron bars. Then I wrote appropriate verses with a magic marker on each stake.

"My son and I installed them together. We had pounded three of them in place and had just finished the fourth when the next-door neighbor walked up to visit a minute. At first it was just the normal sort of stuff neighbors say to each other, shooting the breeze, so to speak. But just before he parted, he added a quick piece of vital information: 'By the way, did you know that the guy who used to live in your house committed suicide?'

"'No, I didn't,' I answered, stunned significantly."

Enough said.

Apparently, not only do demons have assigned *territories*, some may also focus on critical *issues*: abortion, homosexuality, depression, pornography, anger, curses, witchcraft, voodoo, and suicide, just to name a few. If I were Satan, I think I'd put my best guys in Washington DC and in Hollywood—oh wait, maybe that's what he's doing…

> "*The devil* took him to the peak of a very high mountain and *showed him* all the *kingdoms* of *the world* and their glory. '*I will give it all to you,*' *he said.*"
>
> Matthew 4:8-9 (NLT)

Lord, protect my children from any demonic authorities who are out to get them. Intervene when they are attacked. Put the right people around them to provide them a way of escape at the critical moment. Help them to feel Your presence, know your protection, and respond to Your provision for escape. In Jesus's name, amen.

Bill's Conversion

"Anyone who believes and is baptized will be *saved*."

Mark 16:16 (NLT)

You know, when you pray for someone to come to Christ, it doesn't always happen fast. Sometimes it takes years, or even decades. But my prayer for Bill worked quickly. Just a little over a week later, Bill and Carol responded to Christ at the end of a Sunday morning worship. I videoed while Larry baptized. God is good.

Lord, thank You for using me in all my inadequacies to help lead Bill and Carol to Christ. Please put helpful and encouraging people around Bill and Carol for the rest of their lives. Bless them with hope, love, friendship, and many opportunities to share Your goodness. In Jesus's name, amen.

Bill's Epilog

"Love the Lord, all you godly ones! For *the Lord protects* those who are loyal to him, but he harshly punishes the arrogant."

Psalm 31:23 (NLT)

God helped Bill through many financial difficulties. Bill and Carol both got new jobs, moved away, and got a fresh start. They attend church every Sunday and frequently travel to other places to help the less fortunate.

Much later I called Bill just to check on him. I casually asked about whether he had ever sold his old house there.

"I meant to call you," he said excitedly. "It was on the market for four years. We never had one looker or one offer. Then Carol and I prayed over the property like you did for our office. We walked all around. We prayed in every room and every closet—no place was omitted. Then we sold it for cash in just two weeks."

Lord, thank You for the power of prayer. Remind me that my prayers matter, my words make a difference—all because I'm a child of the King. In Jesus's name, amen.

Satan's Tackle Box

Fishing for Men

"Then He said to them, 'Follow Me, and I will make you *fishers of men.*'"

Matthew 4:19 (NKJV)

God sends us to be fishers of men, so Satan sends his followers to do the same. God and Satan are both after the same prize: you. But their plans for you are very different. God reveals His plans for you in Jeremiah 29:

> "I say this because I know what I am planning for you," says the Lord. "I have *good plans for you*, not plans to hurt you. I will give you hope and a good future.'"

Jeremiah 29:11 (NCV)

Satan has other ideas; he is a thief and wants your life for his own:

> "The thief comes only in order to *steal* and *kill* and *destroy*."

John 10:10 (AMP)

He wants to steal your happiness, kill your spirit, and destroy your life. In every possible way.

Both use bait. God's bait is Jesus, peace, hope, eternal life with Him, and rewards beyond your wildest dreams, but Satan's tackle box is very different. He uses the things all around you that you already want every day. He wants you to focus on trinkets (short-lived, temporary things that distract us from the value of deferred gratification and the big picture) rather than true treasures (like a resurrection, a new body, a new earth, an immortal existence, a room in God's own house, etc.).

Lord, open my eyes to the bait I've taken that sucks me in toward the enemy instead of You. In Jesus's name, amen.

Regret

"They shouted loudly and covered their ears and all ran at Stephen. They took him out of the city and began to throw stones at him to kill him. And those who told lies against Stephen left their coats with a young man named Saul."

Acts 7:57-58 (NLT)

Saul—later Paul—fully approved of the stoning of Stephen. He even held the coats of the stone-throwers. He was probably smiling, proud of his little band of dedicated Pharisees. He might have even been the leader, the one who organized the group and laid the plans for it.

But later, after he became a believer in the same Messiah Stephen died for, I am certain he had regrets. Probably nightmares. He had to live with that memory replaying in his conscious and likely his subconscious mind the rest of his life. I'm sure it motivated him on the days when he faced hardships and trials for his faith.

I recently heard of a local man, an East Texas man who committed a heinous act as a young adult and then lived to regret it.

My friend Luke [not his real name] told me that one day he stepped out of his office onto a back porch and found an elderly man smoking a cigar. They began talking, and somehow the subject of forgiveness came up. The story this old gentleman told Luke was shocking. Here it is:

"Luke, I was just a teenager. For thrills, me and my buddies would drive up and down the roads and through darkness all around town. Some in the back of the pickup truck. One guy in the back always had a two-by-four. We would look for people [black people].

I will never forget that night when I was the one with the two-by-four in the back of that truck. I saw a man walking on the side of the road with a dimly lit streetlight. My friend who was driving saw him too. He gunned the motor and raced as close to him as he could without actually running over him. I swung with every ounce of energy and connected perfectly. We all laughed as we saw the board connect and the man tumble over and over on the side of that road.

"I knew I had killed him. I just knew it. There was no way he could have survived—no one could live through that. So the next morning I got up and listened to the morning news, expecting to see a death listed among the headlines. Nothing. I then decided it might take another day or two to make the news. Still nothing. Days became weeks, month, and years. I never heard anything about the man I had hit that night."

"Forty years later, I was sitting in my comfortable living room watching the evening news. I was flipping channels and suddenly saw a reporter interviewing a man in a wheelchair—and immediately I knew this was the man I had hit. He was alive. He had survived the attack and had spent his life in a wheelchair, struggling to survive. The reporter asked him, 'What else would you like to say?'

"The man just looked straight at the camera—and me—and said, 'I would just like to know why. Why did they do this do me?'

"I turned off the television and went to bed, but I didn't sleep a wink. The next morning I called the station and found out where the man lived. It wasn't far. I drove to his house and walked up to the door. I looked at the old door, the broken screen, and the pitiful surroundings. I knocked.

"He slowly made his way to the door and struggled to get it open. He sat in his chair and looked up at me. That old black man said, 'Can I help you?'

101

"I began to pour out my heart, and he invited me in. I told him that I was the one who had hit him. When I finished, I begged him for forgiveness.

"He looked at me with tears in his eyes and rolling down his face. He said, 'I forgive you.'"

That man had spent his life regretting what he did. A lifetime of mental pain, nightmares, and futile attempts to suppress an ugly memory that just wouldn't go away.

Don't live with regret. Make it right.

> "When you offer your gift to God at the altar, and you remember that your brother or sister has something against you, leave your gift there at the altar. Go and **make peace** with that person, and then come and offer your gift."
>
> Matthew 5:23-24 (NCV)

Friends, if you're not willing to reconcile with your brother, then your worship is unacceptable to God. That's a dangerous place to be. Go make it right.

> *Lord, right now I want you to remind me of anyone who has something against me—I've got my pen and paper ready. ... Now give me a willing heart and the right words and courage to make it right. Right now. In Jesus's name, amen.*

Satan Uses Anger

"Don't sin by letting **anger** control you."

Ephesians 4:26

I love basketball. Especially since Jay, my youngest of three sons, loves the game so much. He was once involved in a summer league that played weekend tournaments. So begins the story of my ejection from the game—and the property.

How can a Christian man be bringing glory to God while being ejected from the game of his son? Like this:

We were winning.

The trouble began when I saw the opposing coach pick up the basketball that had rolled to his feet and slam it on the floor. I actually have video proof that it went fourteen feet in the air. Imagine my shock, when the referee—ten feet from that coach and facing him—did not call a technical foul! The entire stadium moaned.

This coach ranted and raved throughout the contest, but the kicker came at the end of the game. It was a three-point game with eleven seconds to go. The same coach who had vented his anger bouncing innocent basketballs high in the air decided to do the unthinkable. He cursed. Loud. Although he was on the opposite side of the court, those ugly words could easily be heard on our side by fans all the way to the top bleachers. I can guarantee you that the administration of that high school would have been appalled, but Saturday morning summer tournaments aren't attended by those folks. No referee should let that go unpunished, but this one did.

The game ended, and I decided someone should stand up for righteousness. I walked up to the ref and said, "It should always be a technical foul when any coach uses profanity. It demeans the integrity of the game." Then I turned to leave, intending to walk to my Jeep and wait for Jay there.

The referee screamed at my back as I walked away. "I can't control what the coach does!" he fumed.

I turned to face him. "It's your job to control him," I responded. He yelled and screamed at the top of his lungs, and I knew it was time to go. This was a battle for integrity that needed to be fought with the tournament director, not the ref who has no problem with coaches using loud profanity.

But the ref was not done with me. As I walked away, he informed me that I was not only ejected from the game, which was over, I was ejected from the property—immediately. I continued to give him an excellent view of my back as I silently walked away. A soft answer turns away wrath, right?

Consider the irony. This man defended the right of a cursing coach to say whatever he wanted. In fact, he said that he couldn't control him. But then he did think he could control me for what I said—after the game was over. He was still giving me orders.

As the yelling continued, I finally turned around and calmly said, "I am going to report you." I turned again to leave. He ran around in front of me, blocking my way, and stood in my path with his fists clinched. I had no choice but to stop. His heavy breathing was about four inches from my face. He said, "Just say one more word and I'll whip your ___. Don't ____ with me."

His anger had taken over. He was no longer rational. He probably wouldn't even remember what he'd said. That's what anger does. It distorts your vision and your memory.

After a big fight, ask the two parties—who both got angry—what happened, and I can guarantee you'll hear two very different stories. Calmness, however, keeps the mind and memory clear and focused. If one person is angry and the other remains calm, you'll get the true picture from the one who stayed relaxed and focused.

> "A person of great understanding is patient, but a short temper is the height of stupidity."
>
> Proverbs 14:29 (GWT)

> "A gentle answer will calm a person's anger, but an unkind answer will cause more anger."
>
> Proverbs 15:1 (NCV)

"A fool gives full vent to his anger, but a wise man keeps himself under control."

Proverbs 29:11 (NIV)

"Control your temper, for anger labels you a fool."

Ecclesiastes 7:9 (NLT)

The New Testament goes even further. It says in Galatians that if you follow the path of anger, you won't be allowed into heaven. Heaven will be a place completely free from anger.

"When you follow the desires of your sinful nature, the results are very clear: sexual immorality, impurity, lustful pleasures, idolatry, sorcery, hostility, quarreling, jealousy, *outbursts of anger*, selfish ambition, dissension, division, envy, drunkenness, wild parties, and other sins like these. Let me tell you again, as I have before, that anyone living that sort of life *will not inherit the Kingdom of God.*"

Galatians 5:19-21 (NLT)

Lord, there have been times in my life when I was just as angry as this referee. I need forgiveness just like he does. Please help me to control my anger and lead others closer to You by showing them kindness and patience. Also, please open this man's eyes to his own weaknesses. Be gentle with him. In Jesus's name, amen.

The Big Lie

"For you are the children of your father the devil, and you love to do the evil things he does. He was a murderer from the beginning. He has always hated the truth, because there is no truth in him. When he lies, it is consistent with his character; for he is a *liar* and the father of lies."

John 8:44 (NLT)

Anger not only distorts the memory; it leads to other, more serious sins.

Two days later, I got a call from the tournament director, just as I expected. She was very kind and polite. She said that she had already discussed the situation with the referee involved.

"Great," I said. "What did he say?" She said that although I had attacked him, he was very proud of himself for not saying a single word to me. He stated that he just turned around and walked away.

Wow. If you decide to tell a lie, I guess you might as well tell a big one.

"These people are hypocrites and liars, and their consciences are dead."

I TIMOTHY 4:2 (NLT)

"But cowards, unbelievers, the corrupt, murderers, the immoral, those who practice witchcraft, idol worshipers, and all liars—their fate is in the fiery lake of burning sulfur. This is the second death."

Revelation 21:8 (NLT)

I told her the truth, and she was shocked. I offered video proof of the actions of the opposing coach to back up my story, but she said that was unnecessary, and fired the ref.

A few weeks later, I got a special gift from Jay on Father's Day that made me proud. He wrote, "I was proud you're my dad at the basketball game. It set an example for me to do the right thing."

Lord, thank you for Jay and for this opportunity to show him how to stand up for truth—even if it's very difficult. Give hi·n the courage to stand up for truth throughout his life. In Jesus's name, amen.

Unforgiveness and Bitterness

"He appeared to two of them as they were fighting, and tried to *reconcile* them, saying, 'Men, you are brethren; why do you wrong one another?'"

Acts 7:26 (NKJV)

Reconciliation. It's the opposite of unforgiveness or bitterness. Webster says it means to restore friendship and harmony.

All of us have been wronged in one way or another. And most of the time the ones who hurt us the most are the ones we are closest too—like our church family, a minister, or a church leader.

John Bevere has written a great book on this subject: *The Bait of Satan.* If someone has offended you, I highly recommend it.

We have all been offended. Sometimes it was unjustified—other times not so much. We're human. We make mistakes. We live in a fallen world. Regardless of whose fault it was, every one of us has been hurt at one time or another.

In fact, if we all sat around and told each other our "offense" stories, we'd all be crying in a few minutes.

Have you ever thought about the fact that Jesus offered forgiveness before anyone asked for it? He also had some very specific instructions about praying for your enemies (sadly, your enemies are often other Christians):

"Love your enemies! Pray for those who persecute you!"

Matthew 5:44 (NLT)

There's probably nothing you can do that makes you look more Christlike than forgiving your enemies and praying for them— even if they never ask. It doesn't free them; it frees you.

> "*Love your enemies!* Do good to them. Lend to them without out expecting to be repaid. Then your reward from heaven will be very great, and *you will truly be acting as children of the Most High, for he is kind to those who are unthankful and wicked.*"
>
> Luke 6:35 (NLT)

You need to also know what will happen to you if you don't. And I'm not talking about eternally; I'm talking about here and now.

I once knew a woman whose husband left her for his secretary. She had married a Christian, and he was a church leader from a fine family. But it happened. I'm not saying it was right for him to leave, but she was what most would call a "whiner." She whined about everything. Constantly. After a while it got old, and he started paying attention to a nice woman who complimented him rather than always complaining and harassing him. It's an old story, as old as the Bible itself.

Anyway, she was all alone and not that old. In other words, she was facing a long future, and she needed to make the best of it—at least for the sake of her children. The family wasn't rich, but she had many conveniences, a nice house, and a mind set on never lowering her lifestyle—in spite of her new lower income bracket. In addition, she squandered and wasted some mutual assets out of spite just prior to the final divorce settlement. What she couldn't see was that hurting him also hurt her.

And that never changed until the day she died. She refused to work because she had been done wrong. She refused to give up regular beauty shop appointments because it kept her from being so sad. She refused to live in a smaller apartment because her husband had run out on her with a younger woman. When she couldn't pay her bills, she called her children. Although they helped her, it hurt every family relationship and every holiday. The list went on and on. In the end, she died penniless, her children only saw her as a burden, and they had to pay for her funeral because she had even exhausted the inheritance her father left her. Her death was a relief to all her friends because they were all tired (for forty years) of hearing how wrongly she had been treated.

In other words, bitterness will eat you up from the inside if you refuse to forgive. It's like cutting your own wrist and expecting the other person to bleed to death.

> *Lord, keep me from bitterness. Give me a heart that's willing to forgive, forget, and move on in joy. In Jesus's name, amen.*

Doubt

> "John the Baptist, who was in prison, heard about all the things the Messiah was doing. So he sent his disciples to ask Jesus, *'Are you the Messiah* we've been expecting, or should we keep looking for someone else?'"
>
> Matthew 11:2-3 (NLT)

Do you ever have doubts? I do. I doubt God's provision (even though I know He promised), I doubt His love (and often feel all alone when I face a problem, and I doubt His commands (why do I think I know a better way?). I've yet to talk to anyone who doesn't doubt some. We're human, right?

Jesus said that John was the greatest human ever born:

> "I tell you the truth, of all who have ever lived, **none is greater than John** the Baptist."
>
> Matthew 11:11 (NLT)

Yet, as we see from the previous verse in this section that when John faced a life situation that didn't match his expectations, he doubted the deity of Christ.

Now let's think about that for a second. John baptized Jesus:

> *"John* agreed to baptize him. After his baptism, as Jesus came up out of the water, the heavens were opened and he *saw the Spirit of God* descending like a dove and settling on him. *And a voice from heaven said, 'This is my dearly loved Son,* who brings me great joy.'"
>
> Matthew 3:15b-17 (NLT)

After he performed the required ritual ("to fulfill all righteousness," Matthew 3:15a), he saw the Spirit descend on Jesus like a dove, and he heard the voice of God from the heavens. The moment Jesus was baptized, God acknowledged Him as His Son. (Perhaps it's the same at our own baptisms.) John saw it all. On top of all this, they were cousins. Mary even visited Elizabeth when they were both pregnant, and John jumped in her womb (Luke 1:41). You have to believe that they shared the prophecies with each other about the sons they carried in their bellies. Notice what the angel told Zacharias that John would accomplish:

> *"He will be great* in the eyes of the Lord. … *He will be filled with the Holy Spirit,* even before his birth. And *he will turn many Israelites to the Lord* their God. *He will be a man with the spirit and power of Elijah. He will prepare the people for the coming of the Lord. He will turn* the *hearts* of the fathers to their children, and he will cause those who are rebellious to accept the wisdom of the godly."
>
> Luke 1:15-17 (NLT)

And notice what the angel told Mary about Jesus:

> *"He will be very great and will be called the Son of the Most High.* The Lord *God will give him the throne of his ancestor David. And he will reign over Israel forever; his Kingdom will never end!"*
>
> Luke 1:32-33 (NLT)

It's also quite plausible that Elizabeth shared all this with John as he grew to adulthood. (By the way, notice the part about Jesus getting David's throne in an eternal kingdom. When did that happen? Answer: It hasn't yet. See my chapter on prophecy in *My Search for the Real Heaven*).

Anyway, if anyone should know if Jesus was "the One," it should be John. He saw the dove and heard God's voice confirming Jesus.

Yet he doubted. When the circumstances of life didn't match what he expected, he doubted. And he sent his disciples to ask Jesus if He was the One.

I have said many times in Bible classes I've taught over the years, "If I were God, I would have sent Jesus when we could video the resurrection and post it on the internet so everyone would be Christians." But then it wouldn't be what? F-A-I-T-H. God wanted it to be a faith issue. He wanted us to choose Jesus of our own free will because we believed.

Remember the days when marriages were arranged by the parents? Children didn't have a choice; the parents chose mates for their youngsters—often times long before they were old enough.

My wife chose me. That made it special. She could have chosen someone else, but she didn't. She chose me.

God didn't make us robots without a choice—although He could have. But if we had no choice but to "love" and "serve" Him, then it really wouldn't be love, would it?

God sent Jesus at just the right time (Romans 5:6), and everyone has a choice whether or not to serve Him. What have you chosen? And remember: if you haven't chosen Jesus then you're not in Christ.

God wants to see if you will have faith. Notice this verse that describes how God tested each new generation of Israelites by leaving some of their enemies free to attack them. Without potential attacks and trials in life, our faith is never revealed:

111

"I will no longer drive out before them any of the nations Joshua left when he died. *I will use them to test Israel* and see whether they will keep the way of the Lord and walk in it as their ancestors did."

Judges 2:21-22 (NIV)

Lord, please forgive all my past doubt, and from now on help me to choose faith when the world makes me doubt. Help me to trust You in spite of what my circumstances look like. In Jesus's name, amen.

Greed

"Don't be greedy, for *a greedy person is an idolater*, worshiping the things of this world."

Colossians 3:5b (NLT)

It's easy to think of idol worship as a thing of the past, but that isn't true. In fact, if anything it's much worse today. We all have our own little "kingdoms," and we're often more focused on our kingdom, our agenda, than God's.

Just one example here: what's your top political priority? In other words what's the number-one issue that will get your vote? Is it the economy (stupid)? Is it who will give you the most money? Is it who will assure your IRAs have the greatest value for your comfortable retirement?

Then you're voting for your kingdom over God's. And one day you'll answer for it, directly to the King, Himself.

Change. Make His priorities yours. Every day.

"*Seek the Kingdom of God above all else*, and live righteously, and he will give you everything you need."

Matthew 6:33 (NLT)

Lord, please forgive me for all the times I've put my kingdom over Yours. And please help me to be different from now on; putting You first; seeking You first; being willing to change my schedule and my vote to put Your agenda above my own. In Jesus's name, amen.

Bankruptcy

"Count the cost. For who would begin construction of a building without first calculating the cost to see if there is enough money to finish it?"

Luke 14:28 (NLT)

There probably isn't a business owner alive who hasn't had fears of failing in that arena. In fact, if you stay in business long enough, that history repeats itself. It's really inevitable—as sure as sunrise in the morning. And, although there are no guarantees of success because you are a Christian, there are some things you can count on.

Satan will attack, trying to get you to worry yourself to death over it—literally.

And God will see you through, no matter what happens.

Others have traveled the same road. I read once that Abraham Lincoln went bankrupt about five times. So did Henry Ford. But look at their legacies: Old Abe is a national treasure and beloved past leader, and Ford was the only car manufacturer who didn't need a bailout the first few years of this millennium. Always remember that whatever you're going through, God will make a way, and this, too, shall pass.

The month after my dad died in 2000, my father-in-law, John Spencer, died. I was as close to him as I was my own father. We had worked together and built the company I had for almost thirty years. Then I discovered that several people in my company had been stealing from me. Immediately after that, I found out we had an accounting error that was enormous; we were accidentally double-counting our inventory assets. Add it all up: total losses were about $500,000.00, an enormous sum. I was so sure we were going bankrupt that I actually started praying that my employees would find good jobs. (The average tenure was over ten years—they were wonderful people to work with.)

I don't know how many Fridays I would sign the paychecks and then the mail would come. I would literally pray over the mail: *Dear God, please let there be $34,567.34 in this stack of mail so those paychecks I just signed don't bounce. In Jesus's name, amen.*

There would be $35,000.00.

The next Friday it might be: *Dear God, I just need $12,347.86 today. In Jesus's name, amen.*

There would be $13,000.00.

On and on it went, Friday after Friday. God made a way.

I lay awake at night and wrestled with the demons. Fear gripped me with an iron fist. I imagined the worst. It made me a different person. Long ago I had learned that when a man is backed into the corner and in a desperate financial situation, he's not the same man. He thinks and does things he wouldn't even consider any other time. Part of that is because men find their identity in their career, and part is because they imagine their whole world crashing down around them; everything they have worked for going up in smoke with no insurance to cover them. Depression, fear, anxiety, dread, anger—it hits them from every side, and they think there's no way out.

But it's all a lie from Satan. Don't listen.

We recovered. Life moved on. God made a way. He owns the cattle on a thousand hills, right? He just sold a few of them and sent me the money. God is good. He'll send you just what you need most right when you need it. He's the God of last-minute surprises, and He loves to surprise you, too. You belong to Him. Rest in that thought.

> *Lord, thank You for having perfect timing. Thank you for giv-*
> *ing me just what I needed at the right moment. Help me to*

use my story and my life to serve You better and enlarge Your kingdom. In Jesus's name, amen.

Suicide

"I lift my hands to you in prayer. I thirst for you as parched land thirsts for rain. Come quickly, Lord, and answer me, for *my depression deepens*. Don't turn away from me, or I will die. Let me hear of your unfailing love each morning, for I am trusting you. Show me where to walk, for I give myself to you. Rescue me from my enemies, Lord; I run to you to hide me."

Psalm 143:6-9 (NLT)

Obviously, I have already covered suicide in Bill's story at the end of chapter 2 and eluded to is in the last item—bankruptcy, but I feel compelled to list it in this section on "Satan's Tackle Box," because it appears to be getting more and more common.

Right now I want to focus on a potential remedy: I call it "R and R." "Relationship and Recounting."

We all need a little "R and R" sometime. Rest and relaxation renews and restores. Reliterally. (I just made that word up, but I like it.)

First, relationships are vital when you face a crisis. You need someone you can tell it to. Everything. Even your worst fears. Just expressing it out loud to a trusted companion makes it seem smaller that it does before.

Second, we need to recount; tell our stories to others. Some call it witnessing. It's a lost art for some, and for others it's something other religious groups do—not us.

Quit thinking that way. Your stories encourage me, and my stories encourage you. Then we can both face tomorrow with greater confidence. Why? Because when I hear how God got you through a great difficulty, I suddenly have more faith in His ability to help me through my own problems. It just happens. I can't explain it any better than that. Just do it.

> *Lord, give us willing hearts to tell our "God Stories" to others. Give us courage to speak up; even it if sounds hokey and weird. Give us the right words in our explanations, and may Your name be glorified in the process. In Jesus's name, amen.*

Blindness

> "In their **blind conceit**, they cannot see how wicked they really are."
>
> Psalm 36:2 (NLT)

If we're ready to be honest, we're all a little blind, especially to our own faults.

I once had a lady working for me named Penelope (not her real name). She was in her fifties, and a pretty good worker. But there was continually some conflict between her and one of the other ladies in the office. Finally I'd had enough. I wanted to help her with this problem—but she was totally unaware that she was the problem.

I called her in for a private meeting. It's never good or kind to criticize someone in front of others. It should always be done in private out of courtesy to the other person.

"What's the problem between you and Sara?" I asked, to get the ball rolling in the right direction.

"It's Sara," she stated flatly. "She is the problem."

"How can that be?" I continued. "Sara has never had a problem with anyone else. But you have. You've had a problem with Sara, Betty, Julie, or Janet. And none of them have ever had one problem with each other. But you have had a problem with every one of them. You, Penelope, are the common denominator," I finished.

She got this shocked look on her face, and she just sat there for a long time. I said nothing.

"Oh," she finally offered. "Maybe it is me. I hadn't thought of that."

She really hadn't, but I had.

From then on Penelope was a different lady. She worked hard to get along with everyone, and, in general, she did. I never had to call her in again. She worked there for close to twenty years in all, several of those at the end of her career. In retrospect, I wish I'd told her that a lot sooner. She would have been happier sooner—and so would I.

Lord, open my eyes to my own faults. Help me to realize exactly what I need to change in me so I can be closer to You. Reveal anything in me that separates us. I want to be closer to You; and more like Jesus. In Jesus's name, amen.

Lack of Bible Study

"All Scripture is God-breathed and is useful for teaching, rebuking, correcting and training in righteousness."

2 Timothy 3:16 (NIV)

When I was a little boy in the early '60s growing up, we had Bible class three times a week for an hour each time. We had a full hour of Bible class before worship on Sunday morning, a second full hour at 5:00 p.m. on Sunday afternoons before worship began at 6:00 p.m., and a third full hour on Wednesday nights. I guess we'll never see another generation get that much Bible study, but you can do it on your own—if you want to.

When my dad died and I began to research heaven because of the great loss I felt in the fall of 2000, I didn't have a lot of spare time. I had three young sons and thirty-two employees. Life was full. But I discovered that if you really want, you can find time to study God's word. I decided I would go to breakfast by myself to study for the first hour of the day, and then I wouldn't make any more lunch appointments so I could study a second hour. I spent two hours a day in God's word for seven years. I literally began to crave that study time; I could hardly wait until it was time to rise in the morning, and for the lunch hour to come. You can read and learn a lot when you spend two hours a day with something. I highly recommend it.

A new generation is beginning to look toward the electronic Bibles that are available today. I love them and have several. My favorite free audio Bible comes through a smartphone app called Bible.Is, which is put out by Faith Comes by Hearing. You can choose any one of over 600 languages available and listen to your heart's desire. My favorite readable version is called the FaithLife Study Bible from Logos. You can hold your finger on a word to highlight it and then choose from a variety of colors, styles, and even intuitive highlighting including blood drops, crosses, hearts, ears, etc. It's awesome. And when you do this, you start to notice new things in the Bible that you never saw before. I highly recommend this to the computer literate folks out there.

One of the things that began to happen as I studied more and more was that I noticed recurring themes. Next, I began to color code these themes with fine point gel pens (they mark smoothly on thin Bible pages and came in packs of colors): black for things about God and His nature, red for things about sin and Satan and spiritual warfare, green for prophecies, fulfilled and unfulfilled, blue for heaven or angels, orange for creation, grey for women, purple for baptism, brown for covenant, and burgundy for things that reveal the literal nature of Scripture. With all these colors filling the pages, the Bible began to come to life. I highly recommend it. You don't have to use my system—invent your own. But I think you'll find that this will help you see things you never would have seen without it.

Regardless, get in God's word. Daily.

Lord, give us a fresh yearning for Your word; a hunger in our hearts. And help us to carve out the time to satisfy that craving. And, Lord, You know what you meant as You wrote the Bible; please help me to know what you mean as I read it. In Jesus's name, amen.

Other Christians

"I am Joseph, your brother, whom you sold into slavery in Egypt."

Genesis 45:4 (NLT)

Joseph's own brothers attacked him and hated him enough to sell him to foreigners without a second thought.

Job's friends are a great example of this. He had just faced the biggest crisis of his life, and all they could do was come accuse him of hidden sin. They told him repeatedly that if he would only admit his sin then he wouldn't have to fear God anymore—or any bad things happening to him:

> *"Put away the sin that is in your hand* and allow no evil to dwell in your tent, then, free of fault, you will lift up your face; you will stand firm and without fear."

Job 11:14-15 (NIV)

Have you ever been attacked by another Christian or a close family member? That really hurts, doesn't it? I finally realized one day why that hurts so much. If someone you don't know very well criticizes you, it's not very painful, but if someone close to you— like your Christian brother—releases a barrage of unbridled fury from his uncontrolled tongue, it hurts. A lot. It's a much deeper pain. The pain is always deeper when the attack comes from your own people:

> "You also have delivered me from *strife with my people.*"

2 Samuel 22:44a (AMP)

When David showed up at the camp of the Israelite army and heard the taunts from Goliath, he was ready to do something about it. He was attacked by his own brother:

> "Goliath, the Philistine champion from Gath, came out from the Philistine ranks. Then David heard him shout his usual taunt to the army of Israel. ... David asked the soldiers standing nearby, '... Who is this pagan Philistine anyway, that he is allowed to defy the armies of the living God?' David's oldest brother, Eliab, heard David talking to the men, he was angry. ... 'What are you doing around here anyway? ... What about those few sheep you're supposed to be taking care of? I know about your pride and deceit."
>
> 1 Samuel 17:23, 26, 28 (NLT)

The sad reality is this: people you trust and love will sometimes attack you. It happened to Joseph. It happened to Moses. It happened to David. It happened to Job, to the apostles, and even to Jesus. If they aren't immune, then neither are you. Work through it, forgive them, and pray for them. People who attack you have suddenly become your enemies, sometimes for no reason. And we are taught to pray for our enemies. Jesus even did that on the cross:

> "Jesus said, '*Father, forgive them, for they don't know what they are doing.*'"
>
> Luke 23:34 (NLT)

Lord, when those closest to me attack me, help me to truly forgive and forget—even before they ask; or even if they never ask. Remind me that forgiveness frees me, not them. And remind me that forgiveness doesn't condone what they did. In Jesus's name, amen.

Success

"Late one afternoon, after his midday rest, David got out of bed and was walking on the roof of the palace. As he looked out over the city, he noticed a woman of unusual beauty taking a bath."

2 Samuel 11:2 (NLT)

Wait a minute. David's army was out fighting the battles for Israel. David didn't go. Wasn't it because he was so busy being king? No. He was lazing around taking naps and getting up in the middle of the afternoon with time on his hands. The phrase, "The idle mind is the devil's workshop" comes to mind. In a big way.

Each of us has a purpose in the kingdom of God, jobs we need to do that we were created for:

"For we are God's masterpiece. *He has created us* anew in Christ Jesus, *so we can do the good things he planned for us long ago.*"

Ephesians 2:10 (NLT)

Here's the verse that explains what David's purpose was:

"Through my servant *David, I will save* my people *Israel from the Philistines and all their enemies.*"

2 Samuel 3:18 (NCV)

David's success gave him a choice. He could stay home, or he could go fight. If he hadn't been so successful, he would have either been dead or still fighting for his life. Your own personal success does the same thing. You can enjoy your success and continue to work in the area where you're gifted, or you can wallow in your success and spend extravagantly, live immorally, and die eternally. It's totally up to you.

As long as David was focused on his purpose and actively fulfilling his purpose, he was happy, healthy, and successful. Over

121

and over the Scriptures explain David's ongoing daily conversational relationship with God. "Should I pursue them, Lord?"

"Yes."

"Should I fight them, Lord?"

"Yes, you will prevail."

"Should I turn left, Lord, or right?"

"Left." God listened and responded to David's direct questions with direct answers. But by the time David had sinned with Bathsheba and killed Uriah, God was talking to David through Nathan the prophet instead of directly to David. Why? The sin in his life had drowned God out. Completely. Is the sin in your life drowning out God? You have the power to change that, and I encourage you to do so. Quickly. Before it's too late. Eternally.

Lord, help me to see the sin in my own life in light of how You are looking at it. Open my eyes to the ugliness of it. Help me to see how it is separating me from You. ... Ok, Lord, now help me to change that. I repent. Show me the way from where I am now to You. In Jesus's name, amen.

Other Modern Idols

"Outside the city are the dogs—the sorcerers, the sexually immoral, the murderers, the idol worshipers, and *all who love to live a lie."*

Revelation 22:15 (NLR)

Right here I want to discuss a few more things that keep us from realizing our true dependence upon God. When it comes right down to it, God provides every breath you take. He gives you every fresh heartbeat. If you're still alive then you still have something He wants you to do for the kingdom. Focus on that. Don't be distracted by fame of success, because you're just one heartbeat away from heaven—or hell.

Insurance. That's right, I said insurance. Insurance is a great thing, but it's easy nowadays to let insurance keep you from realizing your dependence on God. This hit me when I heard a returning missionary say, "You don't need God in America—you've got insurance!" I had never thought about it that way. Car wreck? No problem. Insurance buys you a new one. Probably a better one. Hail damage on a twenty-five-year-old roof? No worries. It probably has hail damage, and then insurance will put a new one on for you. Death in the family? Life goes on—for the spouse, and, in America, it's probably at a higher standard of living than before. Why? Because long ago we decided to buy big policies on ourselves so our families can kick back if we kick the bucket. Bottom line: insurance clouds the truth—that we need God.

Government. Yep, I said government. We depend on the government for all sorts of subsidies, everything from food to rent to cell phones and more. Not just necessities anymore—luxuries. Plus, we expect it. We're mad if we don't get it. We scream and yell and rant and rave that we deserve it. Tornado blow your house away? The government should replace it. Hurricane ruin all your stuff with water damage? The government is responsible. Build a home on a beach and a tidal wave destroys it? You're entitled.

Not.

The government can overspend and borrow for a while, but not forever. Eventually, you have to pay up. You may think you're entitled to an unlimited supply of government benefits, but you're not. Some day the government is going to run out of other people's money to give you. Then who you gonna call?

Position. We spend our time and energy striving for a higher position in our chosen careers instead of striving for relationship with the One who made us. Is that smart, Art?

Possessions. I heard a preacher say on television once, "We ruin our health to gain wealth, then spend our wealth to regain our health. Does that make sense? I don't think so, Joe.

Pleasure. The pursuit of pleasure may be at an all-time high. Your life can't just be about your hobby, Bobby.

Education. Some value education in the things of the world more than education in Bible knowledge, and if these two categories collide, we choose to believe the wisdom of the world over the revelation of the Scriptures. Very sad, Chad.

Power. Some sacrifice all in pursuit of power: family, dignity, health, integrity. That's a no-go, Mo.

Retirement. We see retirement and our saving for it as something that takes precedence over tithing. And if we do tithe (which is very rare today), we do it on net rather than gross income. How do you think God feels about that, Jack?

Sex. Sex, the viewing of it, and the pursuit of it in every possible way has become the daily norm for many American men. Quit it, Schmidt!

Lord, forgive us for putting so many things about serving You and serving and loving our fellow man. Change us from the inside out, and help us to put first things first. Help us to live each and every day in light of eternity. In Jesus's name, amen.

Death

"Those the Lord blesses will possess the land, but those he curses will *die*."

Psalm 37:22 (NLT)

In case you haven't noticed, the overall death rate is 100 percent. I don't care how careful you are with your diet, how faithful you are to your exercise, or how diligently you take your vitamins and see your doc for check ups—you are going to die. Unless Jesus comes first.

I say go ahead and have some butter, enjoy some candy, and eat some bacon. Die happy.

If you're going to die anyway (and you are), why not consider dying for something that matters—like missions? Everyone really wants to be a part of something bigger than themselves, and that's what missions are all about. Don't die for your business, for money, for a bigger home or car, die for people. One hundred years from now, that's all that will matter. No one lies on their dying bed and says, "Man, I wish I had spent more time at the office," or, "If I could only have gotten my financial statement in better shape before I went." As the old adage says, "Hearses don't have trailer hitches."

Live now. Make today count.

Lord, help me to overcome my fear of death. Remind me that death isn't the end for me; it's just a transformation into the real world, the eternal one. Help me to take comfort in the resurrection, and give you my all every single day—no matter what the consequences are. In Jesus's name, amen.

Prayer Hindrances

"In the same way, you husbands must give honor to your wives. Treat your wife with understanding as you live together. She may be weaker than you are, but she is your equal partner in God's gift of new life. **Treat her as you should so your prayers will not be hindered.**"

1 Peter 3:7 (NLT)

Did you know your prayers to God can be hindered by your own actions? It's true. I've never heard a sermon on it, but it's biblical. Forgiveness from God is also conditional. Did you know that?

"But when you are praying, first *forgive* anyone you are holding a grudge against, **so that your Father in heaven will forgive you**r sins, too."

Mark 11:25 (NLT)

Jesus reiterated this in the Lord's Prayer, but, again, no one ever talks about it much:

> "*Forgive us* our sins, *as we have forgiven* those who sin against us."
>
> Matthew 6:12 (NLT)

Think about the wording of this for a minute. Jesus worded it a specific way. Since He is God, and since God invented language, I'm betting He got it right. "Forgive us…as we have forgiven"— past tense. This agrees with the verse in Mark above. Jesus knows that if we are unwilling to forgive, then our own forgiveness is in jeopardy. A scary thought, to say the least.

Bottom line: every one of us has done wrong (sinned), you can't be right with God without His forgiveness, and His forgiveness to you is dependent on your willingness to forgive others. And one more thing: you must be forgiven and clean in God's sight to be effective in removing all demonic entities. They don't have to obey you if you're not in good standing with the King of the universe. In other words it's all up to you. Go forgive somebody. You know you need to. Don't wait.

Lord, help me to have a forgiving heart to all others, just like You have a forgiving heart to me. Help me to truly understand the freedom that produces, the guilt it squashes, the pain it removes—for all of us. In Jesus's name, amen.

God Plans Ahead

My Wife

"A capable, intelligent, and *a virtuous woman*—who is he who can find her? She is far more precious than jewels and her value is far above rubies or pearls."

Proverbs 31:10 (AMP)

We have a poster in the boy's bathroom that they all see when they sit in that special place. It's called, "21 Suggestions For Success," by H. Jackson Brown, Jr. It's a great list of things that will help you live a long, useful, and fulfilling life. It includes things like, "Don't do anything that wouldn't make your Mom proud," and "Understand that happiness is not based on possessions, power, or prestige, but on relationships with people you love and respect." There are also many other items urging kindness, loyalty, honesty, generosity, discipline, and thankfulness—all great suggestions. But do you know what the number one item is on the list? It's, "Marry the right person. This one decision will determine 90 percent of your happiness or misery." Amen.

I also believe that if we ask God for wisdom and discernment in this vital life decision, He will direct us to the spouse that will help us to accomplish our kingdom purpose in this life. I know that's certainly been true in my case. Let me explain.

I tested positive for diabetes in the first grade, but when they retested me, I tested normal. As a child growing up, I never wanted sweets—I always preferred another helping of meat and potatoes. It showed up again in my physical for college. This time it was real. So as I left for college, I had a new problem: dietary. Trying to eat healthy in a college cafeteria at that time was like trying to find a hot fudge sundae with no calories. It was impossible. Every day the menu consisted of something either a) fried, b) greasy, or c) full of fat. My weight shot up along with my blood sugar, and my diabetes changed from "borderline" to "full-blown-insulin-dependent."

Don't get me wrong, I did try to eat right, but it was very hard. My specialist called me into his office one day after a regular check-up. I was barely twenty years old at the time. I will never forget what he said. "Steve," he began, "do you want to live to age thirty?"

"Sure." I chuckled, thinking he was pulling my leg. But he didn't laugh back; he was quite serious. His next words frightened me.

"Well," he continued, "the way you're going, you won't." Stunned is the only word I can think of to describe my feelings at the time.

As I write this book, I'm fifty-five, so you can see I changed my habits, but it wasn't easy. In fact, every single day is a struggle.

When I help churches do an outreach using my book, *My Search for the Real Heaven*, I often tell folks that when they get to heaven if they want to find me, just look for the donut table, because that's where I'll be for the first few decades, catching up on my quota of glazed, chocolate-covered donuts. Thinking back, I realized that I never liked donuts until they told me I shouldn't eat them.

Mary Lynn and I got married after our senior year in college, and she was truly a blessing to my health. She helped get me to be in the habit of eating better and living to see our grandchildren someday. So, be sure you "marry the right person" too. It will make all the difference in the world to your personal future and your mission for God. God plans ahead.

> *Lord, thank You for my sweet wife and how You have used her to make me a better person. Although she has a long way to go, she has worked hard on my training. Give her strength to continue. In Jesus's name, amen.*

My Kidneys

"You did form *my inward parts*; You did knit me together in my mother's womb."

Psalm 139:13 (AMP)

Every day, I pray about my health. Don't you? I thank God for the measure of good health that I enjoy, and I ask for His continued provision in that area for my family as well as myself each day. In fact, I can't remember not praying about my health. And God has answered my prayer in a unique way. I hope that You will be assured of God's involvement in the details of your life as I explain an unusual detail about what He has done for me.

My grandmother was a diabetic. I am a diabetic. I've been on insulin since I was twenty. One of the most common problems with long-term diabetes is kidney failure. Then you must go on dialysis. The kidneys are not like the appendix—you need them every day in order to live.

A few years ago, I had a CT scan because of a small kidney stone. The urologist called and said, "Steve, are you aware you have a duplication on the left hand side?" I had no idea what he was talking about.

I said, "What does that mean, Doc?" Usually, when the doctor uses big words, we tend to mentally extrapolate the problem into a life-threatening, incurable disease.

He responded simply, "You have three kidneys."

Three kidneys. Wait a minute. Most people have two, right? So my first question was, "Doc, does anyone else have three kidneys?"

His response surprised me: "Actually, about 10 percent have a third kidney, but in almost every case, it is non-functional. You have three functioning kidneys!"

Now you need to know that I am a salesman at heart. So I said, "Can I trade one for a pancreas? Let's make a deal here!"

This question seem to surprise the doctor, and he slowly responded, "Well, I guess you could...but then you would be on anti-rejection drugs for the rest of your life, which are worse than insulin shots."

"Never mind," I said. "God must have given me an extra one so I can live long enough to finish my work for Him."

God had planned ahead in the smallest detail of the long-term health needs of Steve Hemphill.

By the way, I couldn't wait to call my wife after I had talked to the doctor! "Hey, babe, guess how many kidneys I have!" God plans ahead.

Lord, thank You for being involved in the daily detailed needs of our lives. In Jesus's name, amen.

My Right Eye

"Jesus reached out and touched him. 'I am willing,' he said. 'Be *healed*!'"

Matthew 8:3 (NLT)

My right eye had started blurring often, and I couldn't get it to focus. It also was watering all the time. I have been an insulin-dependent diabetic for over thirty-five years. The ophthalmologist diagnosed retinopathy in my right eye and sent me to a specialist. Two blood vessels were leaking in my retina that would normally be repaired with laser surgery, which is sort of like repairing a hole in a leaking pipe. However, these leaks were too close to the center of my eye, making it impossible to have surgery. The specialist said that all we could do was wait and see how much leaked. This sort of leak causes permanent vision damage. I asked some Christian friends to pray for the blood vessels to be healed and for the damage to be completely repaired. I thanked then in advance for their prayers.

Two weeks later I visited another specialist in Dallas. This one did a radioactive die test by injecting a bright fluid into my vein and taking pictures of the leaking blood vessels to see exactly where the leaks were. The leaks were completely gone. God is still on the throne, and prayer still works. God plans ahead.

Lord, thank you for listening and responding when we pray for what we need to accomplish our purpose for You and Your Kingdom. Give me exactly what I need to finish the job and come be with You. In Jesus's name, amen.

Fire

"There the angel of the Lord appeared to him in *a blazing fire* from the middle of a bush. Moses stared in amazement. Though the bush was engulfed in flames, *it didn't burn up.*"

Exodus 3:2 (NLT)

Years ago, we had a fire at my office.

The building itself is quite large, almost 11,000 square feet. It's shaped like a big rectangle and covered in thick, grey metal siding. Old, but sturdy and strong. It sits on one of the busiest intersections in our East Texas town of 80,000 on a main thoroughfare. It has a drop ceiling throughout, with a gap between it and the metal roof above.

There had been a terrible drought, and the entire Northeast Texas area was ripe for fires. Making matters worse, there was a large stand of cane growing right behind the building, filling the ravine between our place and the railroad tracks behind it. For those of you who don't know it, dried cane is a ticking time bomb just waiting for a spark to make it explode.

It grows in small segments with a nodule dividing each stalk into neat, separate compartments with nothing inside. So there is a small open cavity between the nodules with nothing but air inside. Since these empty spaces are connected by the nodules to the next segment in that stalk, and since the stalks grow in a cluster closely packed together, one spark that ignites one segment results in an explosion, and it doesn't stop there. The first explosion sparks explosions in the segments above and below, and then to the talk beside it, and the process continues until the whole stand explodes like a chain reaction. The chain reaction continues through the entire stand of cane stalks, and, from a distance, it has the eerie appearance of a nuclear explosion, mushroom cloud and all.

There was a railroad track that bordered the back of my property, and this particular day sparks were apparently flying from one set of wheels that were locked up and skidding down the track, being pushed by the other fifty train cars behind it. One locked-up set of wheels in a group of one hundred cars isn't going to stop the train, is it?

The severe drought that year had the cane pole patch as dry as matchsticks. It caught the grass on fire, the fire raced across to that stand of cane, and there was a huge, thunderous explosion. The employees at Whataburger across the street said it looked just like pictures of a nuclear blast.

I'll never forget sitting at my computer that day, typing away on a project at the opposite end of the building. The thick metal and packed insulation kept me from hearing except a small muffled "boom." I didn't even stop typing. Imagine my surprise just a couple of minutes later when I heard the speaker systems announce, "The building is on fire. Please evacuate immediately." Everything looked and felt fine. I thought it was a joke. But I saw others file by my office, so I decided to join them.

When I got outside I quickly realized it wasn't a joke. Thinking back on it now, it was sort of like an action sequence in a movie when the producer uses slow motion to show you everything that happens to all the characters simultaneously.

Sirens blared as two trucks pulled to the curb on the street side of the building and two more entered the parking lot on the front. It took the four fire trucks about five minutes to get set, extend their ladders, and begin shooting streams of water out onto the roof of the building. I learned later from the fire chief that the attic was within about two minutes of exploding.

From our little huddled group on the opposite side of the parking lot, we could see smoke pouring out of the front left corner of the building. It looked so strange because the explosion of cane was on the corner exactly opposite that spot. At the time, I was relaxed, calm, and secure in the knowledge that I had insurance. Insurance would shield me from true losses, right?

Later I heard a missionary speak who had just returned from a third-world country. He was talking about how churches in the United States were often apathetic about God, church, and religion in general. "In America," he said, "You don't need God anymore—you have insurance!" That had never dawned on me before. Without insurance, I would have been praying like crazy, because everything I had was tied up in that company. I was putting all my faith and trust in something that was about to fail me: insurance. There was a fatal flaw in my policy that I was totally unaware of at the time.

I stood there relaxed, watching the events unfold like you'd watch a segment on the evening news, detached, semi-interested. I had no fear, no worries, I was just calmly thinking through where I'd temporarily house the company while waiting on my big check that would solve every issue. The bankers would tide me over, right? How wrong I was.

One of the salesmen standing next to me said, "Steve, that building is going to burn down." I looked at him and said, "Mark, that's God's building, and if He wants it to burn down for some reason, there is nothing anyone can do to stop Him, including these fire trucks."

Just then I looked up and noticed a small cloud that had formed directly over us. While the fire trucks were struggling to get into position, it started pouring down rain. I walked across the street to Whataburger, and it wasn't raining there. When the hoses began pouring out the water to cool the hot tin roof and put out the fire on the side, the rain stopped, and the little cloud just dissipated.

God's little cloud and short rainstorm saved me from bankruptcy. God plans ahead.

Never forget to pray for God's protection. You never know when that prayer will bring just the right cloud to just the right place at just the right time.

> *Lord, thank You for sending just the right thing at just the right time may times throughout my life. Please continue to do that. And when You do, remind me that it's You. In Jesus's name, amen.*

College Money

> "*God is the one who provides* seed for the farmer and then bread to eat. In the same way, *he will provide and increase your resources* and then produce a great harvest of generosity in you."
>
> 2 Corinthians 9:10 (NLT)

After discovering the huge financial loses (over $500,000.00) I mentioned earlier, I was legitimately worried about funding a Christian education for my three sons. I had attended a Christian school, and although it was expensive, I felt it was definitely worth it. In fact, I had basically saved enough for their education through bonuses I had received over the years from my company that I had paid the taxes on and loaned back for cash flow purposes, planning on getting it out when it came time to pay for their Christian education. It would never happen.

These big losses resulted in major changes in salary and benefits. For over two years, my company couldn't afford to pay me a salary. In place of this, however, I was able to survive and strengthen the financial statement of it by slowly taking out that accumulated savings. When it was finally gone, the financial picture of the company had recovered to the point that it could again afford to pay my old salary. But my nest egg for the boys to go to college on was gone, completely vanished.

My sweet wife, however, offered a workable solution. She would go back to teaching, and her entire paycheck would be for college. So that's what we did. We made it fine, and are even in better shape after they graduated than we were before they started.

One surprising way this worked out to our benefit had to do with how some scholarships are awarded in Texas. I discovered that some schools base the grants awarded to each student on the family's combined salary before the start of that student's freshman year. In other words whatever they qualify for their first year is subsequently awarded to that student for all four years. Since I hadn't drawn a salary for over two years, one son got a $5,000-per-year grant that we would not have qualified for if I had been drawing a salary! So God made a way; He provided $20,000.00 in grants that we weren't expecting that helped us get him through school.

I remembered reading about Corrie tin Boom, who wrote *The Hiding Place*. She described worrying about something when she was a little girl. Her father then said, "Corrie, when you're going to visit your aunt, when do I give you the money for the train ride?"

"Right before I have to buy the ticket," she responded.

"That's how God works; He will give you what you need—just before you need it! Trust Him!"

Lord, thank You for always making a way; even when it seems like the mountain I face is impossible to climb. In Jesus's name, amen.

Marah

"In the second year after Israel's departure from Egypt—
on the twentieth day of the second month[b]—*the cloud
lifted* from the Tabernacle of the Covenant. *So the Israelites
set out* from the wilderness of Sinai *and traveled* on from
place to place *until the cloud stopped* in the wilderness of
Paran."

Numbers 10:11-12 (NLT)

"It was there at *Marah* that the Lord set before them the
following decree as a standard to test their faithfulness to
him."

Exodus 15:25 (NLT)

I always used to think that if I knew for sure that I was traveling the exact path that God wanted me to...that things would
be better; life would be easier, smoother, less bumpy. But then
I noticed an interesting detail about the exodus of Israel from
Egyptian captivity. Let's take a look at this story together. I want
you to pretend you are part of the story, leaving Egypt with all
the other Israelites. Try to experience each step with them, seeing it just like they did—not knowing where they were going
exactly, and not knowing the end of the story. I think you might
see something new. Let's start at the point where they have just
crossed the Red Sea. They have just seen God destroy their enemies in the waters at their back. They know they are following
God. They are absolutely sure of this. He has heard them, He has
delivered them, He has destroyed their enemies, and now He is
leading them on.

First we must remember that they have just witnessed God's
protection during the ten plagues on the Egyptians, and how
God even went so far as to kill every single first-born Egyptian

son while sparing and protecting every single first-born Israeli son. Then they saw God part the waters of the sea when their backs were up against it, and He delivered them when it seemed completely hopeless:

> "The people of Israel had walked through the middle of the sea on dry ground, as the water stood up like a wall on both sides. That is how the Lord rescued Israel from the hand of the Egyptians that day. And the Israelites saw the bodies of the Egyptians washed up on the seashore. When the people of Israel saw the mighty power that the Lord had unleashed against the Egyptians, they were filled with awe before him. They put their faith in the Lord and in his servant Moses."
>
> Exodus 14:29-31 (NLT)

The bottom of the Red Sea wasn't just passable; it was completely dry. Dry means not wet. God can do anything.

The water had stood up—for no reason—on each side of them as they walked through on that dry dirt.

Once they were through and their enemies followed them down between those walls of water (thinking it was safe for them if it had been safe for Israel), the walls had collapsed and killed all their enemies. Wow. What power! What a magnificent event to witness with your own eyes! No wonder that made them "put their faith in the Lord and in his servant Moses"!

Now think about this for a minute. They had witnessed God's power and knew for sure they were following God. No doubt about that. They followed a pillar of cloud by day and a pillar of fire by night. If it didn't move, they didn't move. If it moved, they followed. They were definitely following God.

They were carrying all their possessions plus food and water for the journey. But water is heavy; you can only carry so much. Imagine what it was like three days later, when all the water was gone.

"I'm thirsty, Mommy," the kids would be saying.

"Hold on, child," the moms would reply. "We are following God, and I'm sure He's leading us to some delicious water. We'll be there soon."

Thirsty animals, thirsty children, thirsty everyone. And where does God lead them? Straight to Marah. And what's He going to do there? Test them (Exodus 15:25).

> "They moved out into the desert of Shur. They traveled in this desert for three days without finding any water. When they came to the oasis of Marah, the water was too bitter to drink. So they called the place Marah (which means "bitter")."
>
> Exodus 15:22-23 (NLT)

Three days after leaving the Red Sea, they were completely out of water. They were absolutely certain they were following God. And where did He lead them? To a place with no drinkable water. Now, what would you think? Here are some common modern-day expressions:

"I thought I was following God, but now I'm in a mess, so I must have made a wrong turn."

"I thought I was following God, but He couldn't have led me here."

"I thought I was following God, but if I had been I wouldn't be desperate for help right now."

Wrong. They followed God right to a place where there was no way out but God. God knew He was leading them to a place with no drinkable water. God didn't get there and say, "Whoops, I took a wrong turn," or, "I didn't realize this water wasn't good anymore." No, sir. God knows what He's doing. Always. Read Psalms 139. There are no surprises for God. He made the dirt and the water, and He knows where the good stuff is.

God is still doing that. He is in the business of leading people to a place where there is no way out but God. He does this to see if we will blame Him or trust Him. He does it with individuals, He does it with churches, He does it with families, and He does it with nations. It was a test. It was a test to see if you would blame Him or run to Him.

What will you do? You have a choice. I stand with Joshua: "As for me and my house, we will serve the Lord." No matter what.

Lord, forgive me for blaming You when I reached the bitter water in my life. Remind me that this is a test to see if I'll trust You completely. Help me to pass the test. In Jesus's name, amen.

The Red Sea Was a Prequel to the Jordan River

First Corinthians 10 offers a very interesting insight about this event. As Israel passed below the waterline of the Red Sea, they were being baptized as followers of God's chosen deliverer:

> "I don't want you to forget, dear brothers and sisters, about our ancestors in the wilderness long ago. All of them were guided by a cloud that moved ahead of them, and all of them walked through the sea on dry ground. In the cloud and *in the sea, all of them were baptized* as followers of Moses."
>
> 1 Corinthians 10:1-2 (NLT)

Note also that this momentous event was a prequel to another similar one by the next generation of Israelites forty years later:

> "The riverbed was dry. Then all the people crossed over near the town of Jericho. Meanwhile, the priests who were carrying the Ark of the Lord's Covenant stood on dry ground in the middle of the riverbed as the people passed by. They waited there until the whole nation of Israel had crossed the Jordan on dry ground."
>
> Joshua 3:16-17 (NLT)

Once on the other side, God had Joshua address another critical issue: circumcision. This new generation of Israelites had not been circumcised by their disobedient parents, and this had to be addressed before they could enter the promised land.

"Joshua had to circumcise them because all the men who were old enough to fight in battle when they left Egypt had died in the wilderness. Those who left Egypt had all been circumcised, but none of those born after the Exodus, during the years in the wilderness, had been circumcised. The Israelites had traveled in the wilderness for forty years until all the men who were old enough to fight in battle when they left Egypt had died. For they had disobeyed the Lord, and the Lord vowed he would not let them enter the land he had sworn to give us—a land flowing with milk and honey. So Joshua circumcised their sons—those who had grown up to take their fathers' places—for they had not been circumcised on the way to the Promised Land. After all the males had been circumcised, they rested in the camp until they were healed. Then the Lord said to Joshua, 'Today I have rolled away the shame of your slavery in Egypt.'"

Joshua 5:4-9 (NLT)

One more interesting connection: Colossians 2 calls baptism "spiritual circumcision."

"So you also are complete through your union with Christ, who is the head over every ruler and authority. 'When you came to Christ, you were "circumcised," but not by a physical procedure. Christ performed a spiritual circumcision—the cutting away of your sinful nature. For you were buried with Christ when you were baptized. And with him you were raised to new life because you trusted the mighty power of God, who raised Christ from the dead.'"

Colossians 2:10-12 (NLT)

So baptism is spiritual circumcision, and just as it wasn't optional for Israel, it isn't optional today. We need to be spiritually circumcised (baptized) before entering the promised land (heaven), too. But if it's done without faith, it's just getting wet. Verse 12 there makes that clear: "because you trusted."

Once Israel crossed the Jordan River on dry ground and had circumcised the current generation, they were acknowledged as God's own people and removed their shame (Joshua 5:9 above).

> *Lord, please help me to trust You instead of trusting someone who tells me I don't need to baptized. You know what you meant; You invented language—I trust that You used the right words. Grant me the child-like faith to trust and obey. In Jesus's name, amen.*

God's Uniqueness

> "'This is amazing,' Moses said to himself. 'Why isn't *that bush* burning up? I must go see it.'"
>
> Exodus 3:3 (NLT)

What if Moses had said to other Jews, "When did you have your burning bush experience? Oh, you didn't? My goodness! You're not truly a member of God's family until you've had your burning bush! Let me know when you have it! I am going to be praying that you will reach that level of maturity. Until that happens in your life you're not truly chosen by God; you're incomplete."

Wow! Arrogant. And wrong. There was only one burning bush.

> "You and your fighting men should *march around the town once a day for six days.* Seven priests will walk ahead of the Ark, each carrying a ram's horn. *On the seventh day you are to march around the town seven times, with the priests blowing the horns.* When you hear the priests give one long blast on the rams' horns, have all the people shout as

loud as they can. Then the walls of the town will collapse,
and the people can charge straight into the town.""

Joshua 6:3-5

What if Joshua had said, "Okay, God, thanks! Now I have the
formula for how to conquer Canaan! We will march around each
city once a day for seven days, then seven times on the seventh
day, blow our horns, and the walls will fall out."

Nope. Wrong. There was only one Jericho.

God is the God of surprises. More often than not, last minute
ones. Use my prayers and thoughts as springboards to finding
God at work in unique and wonderful ways throughout your life.
My thoughts and prayers are just examples. Use them to help you
go deeper, soar higher, and know God fuller.

*Lord, open my eyes to all the ways You are at work around me.
Show me who to be. Teach me what to do. Lead me where I
need to go. Reveal Your will to me today—and tomorrow—
and every day. In Jesus's name, amen.*

God's Tests

"These are the nations that the Lord left in the land to
test those Israelites who had not experienced the wars of
Canaan."

Judges 3:1 (NLT)

Have you ever wondered why God didn't just wipe out all the
nations in Canaan instead of commanding Israel to do it? I mean,
really, wasn't that inefficient? Israel had been in slavery for over
four hundred years. These were the most powerful nations on
the planet, living right at the crossroads of civilization. Everyone
from Africa and Middle East had to pass through there to get to
Europe or England, and everyone in Europe or England had to
pass through there to get to Africa or the Middle East (unless

142

they cut through the Mediterranean Sea). There were families of giants there (like Goliath and his family.) If you were going to pick a nation to conquer and destroy the nations living in Canaan, Israel wouldn't be at the top of the list. In fact, they wouldn't even be on the list. At all. It would be like picking a high school beginning wrestler to compete with Hulk Hogan. Odds were against them at every conceivable level. Yet, that's exactly what God did. He picked Israel to conquer them. He did it to show His power to the world. He did it in Egypt, He did it with Israel, and He does it with you and me. God shows His strength through our weaknesses.

God's tests actually do two very important things. One, they demonstrate His power. Two, they test our faith. Are you passing your tests?

> *Lord, help me to see the problems I face as simple tests of faith—even if they are quite difficult. Remind me that there isn't near as much "grey" in Your opinion as there might be in mine. Grant me discernment between good and evil; and help me to always choose the good. In Jesus's name, amen.*

God's Tests Prepare Us

"He did this to *teach* warfare to generations of Israelites who had no experience in battle."

Judges 3:2 (NLT)

Since God was placing His chosen people at the crossroads of the world, do you think it might be important for them to be able to protect themselves against invading armies? Do you think other powerful nations would notice their "land of milk and honey" and want to take it from them? I think so. So God was using their difficulties to train them for battles that would come later.

Do you think God is still doing that today with you and me? I think so.

Lord, help me face my current problems with my learning cap on. Help me to learn everything I need to know from these difficulties so I will be thoroughly prepared to overcome the battles that lie ahead. In Jesus's name, amen.

God's Tests Come through Enemy Attacks

"These are the nations: the Philistines (those living under the *five Philistine rulers*), all the **Canaanites**, the **Sidonians**, and the **Hivites** living in the mountains of Lebanon from Mount Baal-hermon to Lebo-hamath. These people were left to test the Israelites—*to see whether they would obey* the commands the Lord had given to their ancestors through Moses."

Judges 3:3-4

God used mighty nations against Israel to test their obedience. These included five armies of Philistines, several armies of Canaanites, the Sidonian army, and the Hivite army. So it was probably about ten-plus armies of experienced warriors against one small inexperienced army of Jewish newbies who were descendants of four hundred years in slavery. Does the term, "not a fair fight" come to mind?

Again, God is the God of surprises. More often than not, last-minute ones. Do you think He is still using enemies to test our faithfulness today? I do.

Lord, when the odds against me appear to be overwhelming, remind me that with You on my side I've already won. My strength is not sufficient, but Yours certainly is. Thank you for fighting with me. In Jesus's name, amen.

God's Tests of Faithfulness

"You must not intermarry with them. Do not let your daughters and sons marry their sons and daughters."

Deuteronomy 7:3 (NLT)

"Israel lived among the Canaanites, Hittites, Amorites, Perizzites, Hivites, and Jebusites, and *they intermarried with them.* Israelite sons married their daughters, and Israelite daughters were given in marriage to their sons. And the *Israelites served their gods."*

Judges 3:5-6

Israel wasn't supposed to intermarry with the local populace. One of the main reasons for this was because if they did, they would be led astray to follow the local demon gods instead of honoring their covenant with Jehovah God.

Notice first of all that Israel was supposed to wipe out the nations living in Canaan. They disobeyed. They didn't do that.

Notice secondly that by disobeying the initial command they were left vulnerable to disobeying by intermarrying. They disobeyed that, too. They intermarried with these evil idol worshippers.

Notice thirdly that by disobeying these first two commands they were left vulnerable to disobedience of perhaps the most important command of all, a command that was part of the original Ten Commandments: worship and serve no other got but Jehovah God.

That's just how life often works. We disobey in the small things, and it leads to disobedience in the big ones. People stop going to Bible class or midweek services, and the next thing you know, they aren't coming at all.

When your kids are small and they go running full tilt toward the busy street, loving parents yell, "Stop!" Why? Because they were headed in the wrong direction. Many Christians today have quit yelling, "Stop." They don't want to judge. So many children

145

of God have kept running in dangerous directions, and they have ended up venturing into the busy thoroughfare of a dangerous world. We still don't want to judge. Then they get run over and mauled by sin and the terrible consequences of it. And we still won't judge. The fact is: we have stayed silent too long. It's time to speak up for God's truths, before it's too late.

Lord, You have instructed me (a believer) not to yoke myself with unbelievers. Open my eyes to ways I've done that, and help me to untangle myself from them so I can live in obedience to You from here on out. In Jesus's name, amen.

Lines in the Sand

"Don't let evil conquer you, but *conquer evil* by doing good."

Romans 12:21 (NLT)

The story of the battle at the Alamo in Texas as they seceded from Mexico is what I think of when I hear the term, "Line in the sand." Their leader drew a line in the sand and asked every man willing to fight to cross that line. Every man crossed.

God has lines in the sand, too. He wants us to cross the line from apathy to kingdom activity. Daily. Are you standing still, or did you step forward across that line, indicating your willingness to fight for Him? You have a choice. God won't force you to choose life. But I hope you will.

The Ten Commandments are some of God's lines in the sand. God has lines in the sand about entering heaven. Jesus told Nicodemus that unless someone is born of water and the spirit they cannot enter heaven. Baptism is the water birth, but without the heart change—the birth of spirit—it is useless. Both are required for admission to eternity with God.

146

Lord, give me the courage to step across my comfort zone and speak up for You, for truth, and for the kingdom. Help me to do that with grace and kindness. In Jesus's name, amen.

Limits around Mount Sinai

"But you must set a *limit* around the mountain that the people are not to cross. Tell them not to go up on the mountain and not to touch the foot of it. Anyone who touches the mountain must be put to death."

Exodus 19:12 (NCV)

Limits aren't new. God made the universe, so He sets the limits. When you make your own universe, you can set your own limits. Since you currently live in His, you have to go by His limits.

Crossing God's limits have serious consequences. They come in all varieties, but all ultimately end up in the same general place: death. Sinai was no exception. Was the dirt on the mountain side of the limits Moses put up special or life-threatening in some way? No. The fact it that it was the same dirt on both sides. But stepping onto the mountain side was disobedience, and disobedience always leads to death. It was true in Eden, and it's still true today.

Lord, there have been times in my life when I've crossed your limits. Forgive me. Help me to submit to Your instructions from now on in everything. In Jesus's name Amen.

Limits of Gender

"*I allow no woman to teach* or to have authority over men; she is to remain in quietness and keep silence [*in religious assemblies*]. For Adam was first formed, then Eve."

1 Timothy 2:12-13 (AMP)

(The Amplified version is quoted here because it gives greater descriptive detail to the original Greek. Also note that the words in the brackets in this version are part of the text; not added by me.)

In business, there has to be one boss. If a company has two equal bosses, that company has a problem. Things won't get done. Decisions won't get made. There's confusion and chaos and disorientation.

In a family, man has a role, and woman has a role. Neither is more important than the other, but they aren't the same. A woman can't father a child, and a man can't nurse an infant. It's just God's design.

In the assembly, men have a role that's different from the woman. Not better; not more important; not superior; just different. And this is the only place in the Bible where it actually tells why women are not to act with authority in the assembly: because Adam was created first.

I find it interesting that most everyone who wants women to act in an authoritative role in the assembly (when the whole church comes together) use the "cultural" argument. "It's just a different culture today," they often say. In reality, God's reason for the command of silence for women in the assembly is a non-cultural reason. It has to do with the order in which the genders were created. The next verse gives one additional reason:

> "Besides that, Adam was not deceived. It was the woman who was deceived and sinned."
>
> 1 Timothy 2:14 (GWT)

So this passage reveals two reasons for the silence of females in the assembly: Adam was created first, and Eve sinned first. Again, neither is a cultural reason. Just sayin'.

Man has specific instructions from God concerning the assembly, and so does the woman. They aren't the same. Since this passage is so strong on the subject, and since the Bible cannot contradict itself (or it is nullified as the God-breathed inspired word of God), I believe that all other passages should be viewed through this filter.

For example, if another passage says that when women pray and prophesy, they should cover their heads, that cannot mean in the assembly, or the Bible would be contradicting itself, right? Men have put in subtitles throughout the Bible that are not inspired, so men could have put in some wrong subtitles, right? So if the subtitle somewhere says, "Instructions for the Assembly," and the inspired word there says that when women prophesy or pray they should have their heads covered, then that couldn't be in the assembly, right? Please prayerfully consider this idea.

Lord, even if I don't really understand it, help me to obey Your instructions when I come to You to worship. In Jesus's name, amen.

Limits Concerning Worship

"Aaron's sons Nadab and Abihu put coals of fire in their incense burners and sprinkled incense over them. In this way, **they disobeyed the Lord by burning before him the wrong kind of fire**, different than he had commanded. So fire blazed forth from the Lord's presence and burned them up, and they died there before the Lord."

Leviticus 10:1-2 (NLT)

Fire is fire, isn't it? What's the difference? The difference is that God had instructed one thing and these boys had done another.

By the way, I also believe that these two disobedient sons of Aaron had come to lead church after consuming alcohol to an excessive level. At the end of this same chapter, God all of a sudden says:

"You and your descendants must *never drink wine or any other alcoholic drink before going into the Tabernacle.* If you do, you will die."

Leviticus 10:9 (NLT)

Why would God bring that up here if it had nothing to do with what just happened to Nadab and Abihu? Especially because He says never drink alcohol before going to worship, and then ends by saying, "If you do, you will die"! In other words, "If you do what these boys just did, you'll end up dead just like they are." God won't tolerate that.

Lord, help me to worship You in a way that pleases You completely. Reveal anything in me that separates me from You and everything in me that displeases You in any way so I can fix it. In Jesus's name, amen.

Loving the Truth

"*They will die, because they refused to love the truth.* (If they loved the truth, they would be saved.)"

2 Thessalonians 2:10 (NCV)

Truth is important. Very important. Jesus said it would set us free.

"And you will know the truth, and the *truth will set you free.*"

John 8:32 (NLT)

Free from what? Jesus Himself reveals the answer to that just two verses later:

"I tell you the truth, everyone who sins is a slave of *sin.* A slave is not a permanent member of the family, but a son is part of the family forever."

John 8:34-35 (NLT)

Loving the truth makes you a member of God's family! Now that's freedom! If you are a child of God, then you are truly free. Not only that, but you're also an heir, coheir with Jesus Christ! Everyone has sinned, so until they develop a love for truth, they are slave to sin. It actually controls them, owns them, directs their thoughts and moves. It's almost like a demonic trance—and in a way it really is.

I found this verse when my three boys were very young, and never forgot it. When they were small, I used to go into their bedrooms at night and lay my hands on their little heads while they slept. "Lord," I'd pray, "please help Spencer to have a love for the truth so they won't be deceived by a powerful lie and led astray. In Jesus's name, amen." Then I repeated that prayer for Blake and Jay. My greatest fear in life isn't death; it's that my boys might not love the truth and get deceived. Satan is quite good at it.

Lord, help me to have a great love for Your truth. Always. In Jesus's name, amen.

Delusion

"For this reason *God sends them a powerful delusion so that they will believe the lie* and so that all will be condemned who have not believed the truth but have delighted in wickedness."

2 Thessalonians 2:11-12 (NIV)

What happens if you don't love the truth? God is not happy. And that's a very bad thing.

What will He do? He will actually send a powerful delusion so you will believe a lie. Scary stuff. Now you can understand why I prayed this particular prayer for my three sons. It's important to love the truth. Do You?

Lord, nurture in me a total trust for Your word. Don't let me be deceived by man's teachings. In Jesus's name, amen.

The Kind Gentleman

"Your **kindness** will reward you, but your cruelty will destroy you."

Proverbs 11:17 (NLT)

Long ago there was once a kind old gentleman named Jess who lived in a beautiful region. He was loved by all the ladies of the community, respected by all the men, and admired by all the children. He was gentle and loving, wise and kind, generous and patient. Those seeking wisdom camped at his doorstep and waited their turn. Everyone far and wide loved this man deeply— save one. Sate.

Sate hated Jess. He hated how everyone went to Jess when then needed help, advice, or wisdom. He hated the respect Jess had, the friends Jess had, and, most of all, the beautiful land Jess had. As the years went by, Sate's hatred grew. He watched Jess receive honors and awards, and he grew more and more bitter. He nurtured his bitterness like a tender plant that would eventually bear the fruit of eternal life. He lived in his bitterness, and his bitterness and hatred grew bigger and bigger, until he felt he could contain it no longer. That's when it happened—he hatched a plan.

Sate wanted to hurt Jess in a special way, a way that could never be repaired. He didn't want to kill Jess because he wanted Jess to suffer. A quick death would be too easy. He wanted Jess to cry out in unbearable agony—endlessly. So he devised a devilish and cruel plot.

Jess's land was near their city, with spacious hills that gave a spectacular view of the town below, and the largest hill with the best view had many beautiful oak trees. They towered into the sky and stretched out toward each other at the same time. It was almost as if they were the sentinels of the town, looking down at the people with the same caring kindness that Jess possessed. Many of the city dwellers would often pause in their journey to simply stare in awe at the beautiful hill with the gorgeous oaks towering toward heaven.

Sate was scurrying through town one morning as he observed several of the town folk staring up at Jess's beautiful, oak-covered hill when he hatched his devious plan. He decided to sneak onto Jess's hill that night with his axe and chop down the biggest, most beautiful oak—right in the middle. This was sure to injure Jess beyond repair, since these stately oaks were all well over one hundred years old and would never be able to be replaced in Jess's lifetime. This would hurt Jess until the day he died. A perfect plan.

At dusk that evening, Sate, axe and water in hand, stole onto Jess's land to cut that biggest tree in the middle down under the cover of darkness. By morning, he would complete his task, and Jess was sure to be upset beyond comprehension.

Sate worked feverishly through the night, and the darkness hid his ghastly deed. By first light, his work was almost finished. He paused to take a breath and noticed Jess walking toward him in the distance with another man in tow. The mighty oak was still standing, and Sate realized that he must hurry in order to fell the tree before their arrival.

Just as the two men arrived, the tree began to creak and moan. Finally, a thunderous pop signaled the demise of this monument to Jess that began to fall. Sate backed away as the tree fell, but he stepped in a small gofer hole, and failed to make it to safety as the tree fell directly across his body.

As he lay there—dying—he looked up at the kind gentleman walking up with his comrade. His life was slowly ebbing away as Jess leaned in close.

Sate looked in Jess's eyes with great satisfaction and said, "Well, Jess, I may be dying, but I accomplished my goal of hurting you. I cut the biggest, most beautiful tree from the middle of this grove, and it will never look the same. It's marred forever."

Jess's sad eyes of compassion had tears dripping from the corners. "Sate," he said, "if you only understood. My daughter is getting married, and this man with me is the architect I've hired to build her a home—right here. We only had to remove one tree to make room for the house, and you've done it for us.

Sate closed his eyes in agony and drifted off into eternity.

Satan is God's tool to use as He wishes. Everything works together for good for those who are called according to God's purpose (Romans 8:28).

Lord, remind me that no matter how bad the circumstances around me look, no matter how defeated I seem to be, You are the God of surprises—usually last minute ones! Thank You, Lord, In Jesus's name, amen.

George Whitfield

"Truly, O *God* of Israel, our Savior, *you work in mysterious ways.*"

Isaiah 45:15 (NLT)

"The great evangelist of the 18th century George Whitfield was once robbed in such a way that it spoke of the goodness of God. Once when he was riding to a meeting with another man, a robber met them on the road and demanded all their money. The cocked pistol in his hand was argument enough, and the two did as the robber insisted. The robber left, and the two continued on. In a few moments, the robber returned and demanded Whitfield's coat, saying, 'It is better than mine.' Once again, the preacher did as he was told. With a smirk, the thief threw his old coat to Whitfield and rode away again.

"As Whitfield and his friend continued on their journey, they looked behind them only to see the robber riding at full gallop toward them again. Deciding enough was enough, the two spurred their horses and reached the next town safely before the robber reached them. Later they wondered why the thief tried to get them a third time, but when Whitfield felt the lining of

the thief's coat, he found the answer: Inside was a purse with many times more money in it than the thief had taken. Whitfield used the money for the orphans that he supported in Georgia."
Tempered Steel, by Steve Farrar

> *Lord, all things and all people are in Your power—the good people and the bad. Use us all to accomplish Your purposes. In Jesus's name, amen.*

Tony's Banking Problem

"Do not be mean-spirited and refuse someone a loan because **the year for canceling debts is close at hand.**"

Deuteronomy 15:9 (NLT)

Tony is a good friend. He grew up about ninety minutes from here and had an uncle who was a dentist and had a substantial amount of money. The uncle invested wisely, and it grew more. He bought a bank. And he was glad to help his beloved nephew, Tony, by loaning him a substantial amount to purchase some automobile dealerships.

Tony was also a smart businessman—just like his uncle. He became a Christian and was very active in his church. Everyone loved Tony. He was always helping people—he never turned a deaf ear to someone in need. God blessed Tony's businesses, and life was good. He bought a lake house, took nice vacations, and spent a lot of quality family time with his wife and kids. He prayed often, was vocal in the work environment about his Christianity, and generally did everything he could to nudge others toward Christ. A man to admire, to say the least.

But then things went south. The economy crashed, General Motors was in crisis, and word on the street was that a large number of dealerships were going to be eliminated. Not only would some of his automobile businesses going to be randomly cut off—in spite of their good reputation and great payment record, never missing a payment or even being late—but in addition to that, he would still owe his Uncle the rest of what he had borrowed to purchase them in the first place.

Tony asked his closest friends for prayers. Things looked tough—but they were about to get much tougher.

Next, Tony's uncle sold the bank. Perhaps he was ready to "hang it up," but for whatever reason, he was ready to get out of the banking business and all the headaches that appeared to be on the horizon because of the financial crisis.

To make matters worse, the new bank owners—in light of the difficulties of the car business at the time—had made a corporate decision to dump all the loans of that type. That meant they were calling all the loans. It would be like your mortgage company giving you a call when you still owed a substantial amount on your home and saying, "We don't do home loans anymore. We are calling the loan, and want you to know you have three months to pay it off." You have got to be kidding. But that's what basically happened to Tony.

It didn't matter that Tony always paid on time. It didn't matter that Tony always paid more than required. It didn't matter that Tony was honest, hard working, and easy to deal with.

It also didn't matter to the new bankers that Tony was a Christian. But it did to Tony. He wanted to do the right thing, honor Christ in all his actions, and continue supporting his family.

Under Tony's calculated leadership, his dealerships had grown quickly, expanded their customer base, and paid their notes like clockwork. But fast growth also means more need for capital, and the floor plan all dealers work under meant that the inventory on the lot was leveraged. This meant that if he couldn't work something out, the cars on his lot might just be picked up one day and taken to other dealers. How would you like to try to sell cars you don't have? Impossible, right? That's the sort of situation Tony faced.

To help you get the proper perspective and scale on this sort of problem, let me explain how drastically business changed when the economy crashed. In 2007, before the crash, the total number of annual new and used cars sales was about 18 million per year. Overnight—literally—that number was cut in half. How would you like to have to adjust your business plan to handle that kind of change? And remember, his bank loans didn't change. You owe the same amount and have to make the same monthly payments with only half the revenue you were making on them yesterday.

It's times like this when you really learn to pray and trust God. Tony had nothing to do with the changes, but he had to deal with them. He had to survive. His family and his employees were counting on him. Try to live with that kind of stress. It's not easy, I can assure you.

At the time, Tony's total debt was about $9 million. A staggering number. Would you be able to sleep at night if the note got called? I confess, it would test my faith. It would be easy for me to just throw up my hands and give up.

Not Tony.

He studied his Bible. He prayed fervently and often. And he trusted God. You won't believe what happened.

The first hurdle was being allowed to keep the dealerships. Rumor was that some of Tony's were on the "hit list," and that FedEx letters were going out to the ones being closed. They were supposed to arrive on a certain day. Everyone was on pins and needles. FedEx came and went. A sigh of relief. But thirty minutes later the FedEx truck circled back. They held their breath again: just more parts. Whew! They'd made the cut, in spite of what they were told.

One down.

But then the new bank was so unreasonable, as they continued to threaten to come take one of the locations because its loan was due that Tony finally said in desperation, "Come get it. We'll give you the keys. It's yours. Good luck." They backed down and gave him a little more time to work something out. (They really didn't want to be in the car business. They just wanted their money.)

The new bankers were more and more desperate to get out of the auto industry. Tony had found funding for $5 million of the debt, but couldn't get help for the remaining $4 million. Finally one day they sent word that if Tony could find funding for $3 million, they would settle for that much. At first he couldn't believe his ears. "You mean even though I owe you $4 million, if I pay you $3 million in the next sixty days you'll call it even? You won't ask for the rest? You'd give me a 25-percent discount?" They said yes. (Even people with money are stupid sometimes, I guess.)

Tony found a local bank happy to fund a dealer with 25 percent less debt than he had the day before. He got the financing and sat dumbfounded. God had turned a hopeless situation into a big blessing. And with 25 percent less debt, Tony was in better shape than he ever had before. Prayer still works.

Lord, when my own situation looks completely hopeless, remind me that You are in control and that You can do anything. Literally. In Jesus's name, amen.

Life Was Calm

"It is not that we think we are qualified to do anything on our own. Our qualification comes from God."

2 Corinthians 3:5 (NLT)

It was hot. It was August in East Texas. Humid, but tolerable—if you've lived here awhile and gotten your body acclimated to the sultry weather. Life had finally settled down from the frenzied pace, the declining US economy, and a lifetime of having raised three active sons.

I had become a reluctant author. I got talked into writing a book about heaven.

Dad had died, and the pain of his loss had led me to study every verse in the Bible about heaven. The details of that study filled a book with over 75,000 words, and that was the total after I had taken out 15,000 at the request of my publisher.

I enjoyed the study immensely, but I've always been a very active, energetic person, so the thought of actually sitting still long enough to write a book had zero appeal to me. Just as Jonah ran away from Nineveh, I ran from that book project. But God had a different idea. So, I relented. I wrote it. It took about seven years, but I wrote it. Then I was ready to submit it. But there was a problem: I was clueless about the book industry.

First, I went through my personal library, writing down the web address of every publisher with books that appeared to be similar to mine. That made sense: if they publish books like the one I'd just written, then they would be the perfect fit.

Lo, it was not to be. When I visited their web sites I made a startling discovery: none of them—zero—accepted "unsolicited manuscripts." (A writing term I had just learned.)

You had to "be somebody" or "know somebody" to get published. I didn't qualify on either account.

Lord, I know I'm not qualified to be much help to You and Your kingdom, but please—use me anyway. In Jesus's name, amen.

Two Aces—Not

"If you are kind only to your *friends*, how are you different from anyone else? Even pagans do that."

Matthew 5:47 (NLT)

After realizing how difficult it is to get published, it dawned on me that God already had a plan. Years ago He had given me two "aces." That must be how He was planning to get my book published.

My first "ace" was that I was friends with an author. I went to school with someone who became successful as a writer. He wasn't a bosom buddy, but he definitely was a friend—one who would remember me and spoke kindly every time we ran into each other.

In addition, my wife was a friend of his wife. They grew up knowing each other at church camp. Since I had dedicated part of the money from my heaven book to benefit that camp, I was even more hopeful he might lend a hand by being willing to write an endorsement that would appear on the cover. And since he was successful, my book would have a greater chance for success with his endorsement.

I just knew this was how God would provide a way for my work to be published. I printed a copy of my yet unpublished draft of *My search for the Real Heaven* and put it in the mail with a long letter, asking if he would be willing to write an endorsement. He was very kind but too busy to assist me in this project.

Another friend had a connection with a famous personality, so this was my second potential "ace in the hole," but he was uncomfortable asking them for assistance.

Now I was really getting discouraged. But, God had led me here, hadn't he? Maybe I should go to battle in the spiritual realm and put this problem at the feet of the King.

Revelation 3:7 says, "When he opens a door, no one can close it. And when he closes it, no one can open it" (NCV).

I actually wrote this prayer about a week before I finished my book on heaven in the summer of 2008:

"Lord," I wrote in my prayer journal, "I wrote the book. But I'm at a brick wall. So if You want it published, I'm asking You to open a door. You're the One Who opens doors no one can shut, and shuts doors no one else can open, so I'm laying this problem at Your feet. In Jesus's name, amen."

An Unsolicited Manuscript

"I was found by people who were not looking for me. I showed myself to those who were not asking for me."

Romans 10:20 (NLT)

By this point, I found that the publishing industry had a special name for my writing. It's called an unsolicited manuscript. You know what that means? It means "They ain't asked for it, and they not fixin' to."

But I was also sure this is what God wanted me to do. So I moved forward in faith.

> *Lord, I'm a "nobody." But as I read the Bible, it looks to me like You often use "nobodies" like me. So I am making myself available for Your use and Your schedule. Use me to Your glory. Give me the energy, resources, and strength to accomplish what You want me to. In Jesus's name, amen.*

Did God Respond?

"I am the one who answers your prayers and cares for you. I am like a tree that is always green; all your fruit comes from me."

Hosea 14:8 (NLT)

Did God respond? Yes. In a dramatic way.

I finished writing on a Friday afternoon. I went in to my office on Monday morning and got busy with my normal, daily activities, put out a few office "fires," and was finally ready by mid-afternoon to search the web for "publishers who accept unsolicited manuscripts."

To my surprise, several possibilities appeared on the screen in front of me. Near the top of the Google summary was a link that caught my eye: TatePublishing.com. I clicked. The screen changed, and a quite impressive web site appeared. It looked very

161

professional. It wasn't a self-publish company, and the site was user-friendly and Christian oriented. I noticed that they published all kinds of books including lots of children's books, but also that they seemed to be oriented toward Christian reading material. It looked perfect. The more I read and explored, the more excited I got. There were video clips and quick links to their authors, their staff, and their corporate accomplishments.

They were located in Mustang, Oklahoma, very near Oklahoma City, and they had great accolades from the Oklahoma Chamber of Commerce. Twice they had been voted the "Best Business in the State of Oklahoma to Work For." I'm sure it was worded differently, but that was the gist of it. I read on.

It turned out they tithed as a company. This really impressed me, since their sales were over $160 million per year. They also had invested in their own printing presses. Most publishers farm out the printing, but not Tate. Having their own printing facility speeds up the publishing process. It shortens the whole process from about two years to less than one year.

Additionally, they had no debt whatsoever. They give to organizations that help the poor and underprivileged, including literacy programs and other similar groups. Now they really had my attention.

I didn't have time to research lots and lots of publishers who accepted "unsolicited manuscripts," so I attached my work as a pdf and hit the send key. By now, it was after 5:00 p.m. and time for me to get home to the family. As I got up to leave, a window popped up on my screen. It was a video of a man in a nice suit. "Hello," he began, "I'm Dr. Richard Tate, founder and owner of Tate Publishing. Thank you for submitting your manuscript to us today. We'd like to get to know our potential new authors, so please pick up the phone right now and call me at 1-800-..." So, I did.

I got right through to him, and we had a nice, long conversation. He asked me about my writing and what had motivated me, listening attentively to my answers. Finally, he said, "Steve, my editing department is about nine weeks behind on reading all the submissions, but I'm moving you to the top of the list. We will look at your work first thing tomorrow morning, and if we think we can sell ____ books, we'll offer you a contract."

In just forty-eight hours, I had a contract offer in a FEDEX package on my front porch. I saw this as simply another "God thing."

Lord, thank You for opening doors that no one else can open, and shutting others that no one else can shut. Help me to remember daily that You—and only You—are the reason for my success, my life, my every breath. In Jesus's name, amen.

Meeting Dr. Richard Tate

"They met with the king regularly and held the highest positions in the empire."

Esther 1:14 (NLT)

I will never forget the day I drove to Mustang, OK, to visit the facilities of Tate Publishing & Enterprises.

A friend took the day off and drove to Mustang with me, someone who knows contracts. I asked him to review my offer on the way and help me evaluate Tate as a company. In the car on the way he finished reading the contract and said, "Steve, this looks great. There's no reason not to do this." One more confirmation I was on the right track—God's track for me.

I had a 2:00- p.m. appointment, and when we pulled up to the nice brick building housing the headquarters of Tate, there were only two parking spots open. One was right by the front door entrance, and was marked with a large sign. It reminded me of those "Employee of the month" parking places reserved for the worker with the best attitude or sales record, so I started to pass it by for one just across from it, a little farther from the entrance. But as I glanced back at the sign, I was shocked by what was posted: "Reserved for Author, Steve Hemphill." I never felt so special. I backed up, pulled right up into that place in my four-door Jeep, got out to stand beside the sign, and said to my friend, "Take my picture." I felt like a little boy again. I used to do that when I was about five when our family when on vacations. "Take my picture, Mommy." And she would. I smiled my biggest smile then, just as I did in front of that parking spot—reserved just for me. I felt like I was on top of the world, ready to get to work for God.

Lord, thank you for sending me to the right place at the right time so I could help make a difference in Your kingdom. In Jesus's name, amen.

My Search for the Real Heaven

"I devoted myself to search for understanding and to explore
by wisdom everything being done under *heaven."*

Ecclesiastes 1:13 (NLT)

Most people don't realize that you don't always get to name your
book what you want to. I had named my "unsolicited manuscript"
"Glimpses of Heaven." But a short time before my book was cop-
yrighted, someone else used that name. So when the time came
to determine what I would call my manuscript, many possibilities were considered. When I finally settled on *My Search for the
Real Heaven,* I was much happier with that name than I was my
original title. I also believe this to be a God thing, since another
popular book about heaven was soon to be published: *Heaven
Is for Real,* a great little book that quickly became a best-seller.
Since mine also had the words, "Real," and "Heaven" in the title,
my sales were probably helped by this other excellent work.

Now there are several books out about heaven. In fact, I'm
hoping that one day the bookstores actually do have a "Heaven"
section. You never know.

This makes me think of it like the section of town that has
lots of restaurants where everyone goes to eat. They all sort of
feed off of each other's success. I might drive to go eat at a steak
house, and then notice the seafood place next door, and then
turn in at the seafood place because the steak place was packed.
Next time, when the seafood place is full, I eat steak, avoiding the

crowd. Hopefully there will one day be a whole section of books on heaven at the bookstores. I'm hungry for heaven, aren't you?

Lord, You devoted yourself to me—now help me as I devote myself to You. In Jesus's name, amen.

The Contract Offer

"In the same way, he took the cup of wine after supper, saying, 'This cup is *the new covenant* between God and his people—*an agreement confirmed with my blood.* Do this to remember me as often as you drink it.'"

1 Corinthians 11:25 (NLT)

I want to reveal something that I didn't talk about for a long time. It has to do with the things I found in the Scriptures about heaven. I was so surprised by what I found in the Bible about heaven that I actually prayed this prayer: "Lord, I don't want to lead anyone astray, so if what I have concluded about heaven is a lie, if it isn't the truth, then defeat me. Don't let me get a book contract offer. In Jesus's name, amen." Then I got an offer only forty-eight hours after submitting it. What would you conclude about that?

The reason I haven't told that before is because I didn't want people to get the wrong idea, but that's exactly what happened, and I can't change that. We don't have to agree on every aspect of heaven, but that's how God responded to my prayer. And if you think about it, I asked for the opposite of a sign. I could have asked it like this: "Lord, if what I found is the truth, then help me to get a book contract in forty-eight hours." That would have been putting God to the test. But I asked God to do what was easy, what normally happens. Most people do not get book contracts. I had asked him to make happen what usually happens: nothing.

So to me, that makes this all the more amazing. But then, we serve an amazing God, don't we?

When I read the contract from Tate Publishing, I almost fainted. It was about twenty-one pages in length, with all but one page covering the legal details: time lines, commission rates for hard copies, eBooks, Nook Books, iBooks, and Kindle versions. But the last page was their statement of faith as a publisher. It went something like this: "We believe in the Bible as the inerrant word of God, we believe Jesus is the only way to heaven, we believe in the Lord's Supper, and we believe in baptism."

I don't know about you, but I had never seen "baptism" or the "Lord's Supper" in a legal contract before. Have you?

Lord, thank You for sending me to a company with godly people and godly principles. Please bless Tate Publishing greatly as they work to help further Your kingdom. In Jesus's name, amen.

Prayer Made the Difference

"When Job prayed for his friends, the Lord restored his fortunes. In fact, the Lord gave him twice as much as before!"

Job 42:10 (NLT)

I own a copier business in Longview, Texas. We also serve Mt. Pleasant. One day, I got a call from a ministry outreach there that had recently leased a new machine on a three-year lease. Sam was quite upset on the phone and wanted his machine picked up as soon as possible. He said, "Your salesman promised that we could cancel this lease at any time, so I'm calling now to get it picked up." I took down his number and promised to locate his paperwork and call right back.

I discovered he was six months into a three-year lease and that he was four payments behind. In addition, he owed us over $300 in service and supply charges. It seemed obvious to me that he was in a bind financially, but there wasn't much I could do at that moment. We had already been paid by the leasing company, and he owed them the balance of the payments.

I returned his call, armed with this new information, and was greeted by a rather cold response. I apologized that he had the misconception that he could cancel at any time, because we go to great lengths to train our salespeople NOT to say that. However, since I was now aware that he needed out, I promised to make every effort to find someone else to take over the payments for him, thus relieving him of the obligation. He then asked what I was going to do for him "today." I suggested that all I could do "today" was recommend that he catch up on his payments, since he was four payments behind.

His response was curt and rude. He said, "I have already talked to my lawyer about your salesman's promise, and he said that it was definitely a verbal contract. So you will be hearing from my lawyer SOON!"

"Okay," I said, "but before we hang up and you go see your lawyer…you're in the ministry, right?"

"Right," he said. I asked if we could pray about it together on the phone before we hung up. He said, "…Okay…" I have been in situations before where conflict was involved and the other person offered to pray, and they prayed a very condescending prayer.

So I said, "I'll tell you what, I will start the prayer, and you can finish it." He agreed.

"Dear God," I prayed, "please bless Sam in his ministry work there in Mt. Pleasant. I feel like he is in some financial trouble right now, and I pray that whatever you want him to learn from this that he will learn QUICKLY, so that his life, his work, and his ministry can be a blessing to you. And if I have done anything wrong or unfairly, I pray that you will put it on my heart to make that right. In Jesus's name…."

There was a short pause, then I heard Sam quietly say, "God, I agree with everything he said. In Jesus's name, amen."

I never heard from Sam again *or* his lawyer. And he paid us for the toner. Prayer worked…again.

> *Lord, whenever I'm confronted with a new problem help me*
> *to make prayer my first response instead of my last. Give me*

*wisdom in those moments and a reminder to seek Your will. In
Jesus's name, amen.*

Prayer of Desperation

"Nebuchadnezzar flew into a rage and ordered that
Shadrach, Meshach, and Abednego be brought before
him. ... 'I will give you one more chance to bow down
and worship the statue I have made ... But if you refuse,
you will be thrown immediately into the blazing furnace.
And then what god will be able to rescue you from my
power?' Shadrach, Meshach, and Abednego replied, 'O
Nebuchadnezzar, we do not need to defend ourselves
before you. If we are thrown into the blazing furnace, the
God whom we serve is able to save us. He will rescue us
from your power, Your Majesty. But even if he doesn't, we
want to make it clear to you, Your Majesty, that *we will
never serve your gods* or worship the gold statue you have
set up."

Daniel 3:13-18 (NLT, selected parts)

Billy, a close friend of mine, owns a title company in the metro-
plex. Billy helped promote my first book, and we have a long
business relationship that developed into a close friendship. If
I needed prayer for something today, he's one of the first people I would call—even though we don't go to the same "brand"
of church.

The following story was on the six-o'clock East Texas News
one day, but only the overview was detailed—an elderly man was
fishing alone on a local lake, fell out of his boat, and was rescued
after five hours of clinging to a small branch near the surface, far
from shore in the dark.

Billy forwarded me an email a few days later that gave the
details, because the elderly man was the father of one of Billy's
employees, Jeff. Here's the story in Jeff's own words:

"My Dad called me yesterday and told me that on Monday, while fishing on Lake Ray Hubbard, he fell off his boat in twenty-foot waters and hung desperately to a tree branch sticking about ten inches out of the water for the next five hours. His trolling motor was running when he fell overboard so his boat just kept on going. He was about 250 yards from shore and knew he could not make the swim, so he prayed for a boat. He found a small foot hold on the branch that allowed him to raise up to about his chest where he would holler for help once every ten minutes to help conserve his energy, and he prayed for a boat. After five hours in the water and with nightfall approaching, he made the assumption that he would not survive his ordeal. He took his belt off, and tied himself to the tree trunk so that we would be able to find his body, and he prayed for a boat. Now when a person makes a decision like that, you have to know that the situation is as serious as it can get. He told me that he spent all of that time talking with Jesus and praying for a boat. He said 'Lord, I'm not going to make any crazy promises to you that I can't keep to get me out of this mess, and if this is your will, then I accept it, but I will hang on as long as I can, and keep praying for a boat.' My dad told me after his ordeal that his greatest blessing came in knowing that he didn't come to know Jesus for the first time while hanging on to that tree. When he got in his car that morning, when he left the marina, when he fell in to the water, Jesus was right there with him.

An eleven-year-old boy on the shore heard my dad's screams for help. He told his mother, who looked through a pair of binoculars and saw my dad's empty boat and called 911. Just as darkness was setting in, my dad saw a helicopter and began waving his arms. As the helicopter circled above, all of Dad's attention was so focused on the helicopter that he didn't even notice the fireman behind him on a jet ski or the Dallas rescue boat coming toward him. My father spent five hours clinging to life on a small branch praying for a boat. Our Heavenly Father sent a helicopter, a jet ski, and a boat to rescue him, all after sending His son Jesus to save him. God is so good."

Lord, thank You for rescuing us in our time of trouble. Thank You for coming through just in the nick of time—just like you did all through the Bible. But remind me, Lord, to have the attitude of Jeff's dad—and of Shadrach, Meshach, and Abednego: You are able to deliver and rescue me, but if You don't, You're still God. And I won't bow to the idols of this world. In Jesus's name, amen.

Pilgrims

"*The Lord is a faithful God.* Blessed are those who wait for his help."

Isaiah 30:18b

Years before I began my research on the topic of heaven, I taught classes at church on the topic of spiritual warfare. I probably accumulated over six hundred PowerPoint slides on the subject. When our family changed churches about a decade ago, I began teaching a whole new group of classes at our new congregation on this topic. Finally I had taught the topic to the high school, junior high, and every adult class except one: the young marrieds.

One of the class leaders for that group approached me one day in the Summer of 2008 and asked if I'd be willing to be their teacher that fall on the subject of spiritual warfare.

"Sure," I said, "but I have one condition: I want you guys to pray for me. Satan does not want you to know this stuff. Every single time I teach it, something bad happens to me."

"Okay," was the response I got, but I could tell he wasn't convinced.

Four weeks into that quarter, my biggest customer, Pilgrims Pride (a multi-billion-dollar chicken company) went bankrupt, owing me $210,000.

"See," I told them the following Sunday, "I told you Satan didn't want you to know this stuff. I told you I would need your prayers."

Wide-eyed, they almost nodded in unison. Now they believed me.

Big accounts like Pilgrims were good and bad. It was good to get orders for $50,000 to $400,000 per month, but bad in that they paid slowly. Once, in fact, they sent us a letter that basically said, "Don't even call us unless we are over sixty days past due." So we had a separate line of credit just for the Pilgrims account. I borrowed against what they owed us on a regular basis. As they got slower and slower to pay (preparing to go bankrupt, I guess), I eventually maxed out the line.

During the month before their filing I had called to ask for payment because about $100,000 of it was over twelve months past due! They responded with cordial friendliness, but after looking up the invoices I had called about, they responded with, "Steve, those bills are over twelve months old. That's two budgets ago! I don't know how we are going to pay for those."

"Neither do I," I responded, "but you certainly owe it. I delivered the products, and we need the money." They promised to do what they could, and we hung up.

Then the bombshell—out of business. As most of you business people know, in this sort of situation you usually get about a dime on the dollar—if you're lucky. Sometimes you don't get anything.

Now you can imagine my thought process: we had weathered the storm of losing about half a million a few years before, but with another $210,000 in losses staring me in the face, I felt like it was now just a matter of time until it was all over. The company literally couldn't stand another round of losses that significant. On top of that, I now had to make interest payments monthly on the $210,000 they owed. Fortunately, I had a great Christian banker, and they were patient and supportive.

Now there was another issue: returning the last check Pilgrims had sent the week before for $60,000. I always got confused when we occasionally had a customer go bankrupt; I forget the difference between chapter 7 and chapter 11, but I found out something brand new with the Pilgrims situation: if they have paid you any money in the sixty days prior to filing, they have the legal right to ask for the money back! I can tell you one thing for sure: that $60,000 wasn't just sitting in the bank waiting to be requisitioned. It was spent on payroll and accounts payable. It was gone, bro.

The class prayed, and I never got the request for the money to be returned. Prayer still works.

Then it was like time stood still for me for over a year. No word from Pilgrims. No demands from the bank. Fridays came and Fridays went; just enough came in for the bills and the pay-roll, week after week. I woke up at night sometime, wondering how I would handle it when the word finally came down that we wouldn't get all our money. That wasn't how things always worked in this situation. You got a dime on the dollar, or twenty cents if you were lucky. I knew we couldn't handle it. I was barely making the interest payments. I cried some but mostly tried to hide my pain and fears from my family and friends—especially the church ones. That would show a lack of faith, right? And I was a dea-con; deacons were tough and strong, like linebackers on a football team. The church was my team, and they needed me to be tough, right? Bottom line: all sorts of lies like that swirled around in my head off and on for over a year.

A year is a long time to wait for an answer. But I had no choice.

In fact, during this same time—when I could least afford it—I also had a frivolous lawsuit. I had done nothing wrong, which came out in the end, but I spent over $60,000 in legal fees, depo-sitions, and lawyer time to prove it. When it rains, it pours, right? It was pouring on my life in what seemed like every possible way.

Looking back, I probably wasn't very warm and cuddly to live with. I am very grateful for my family's patience and kindness toward me through all these difficulties—in spite of my curt responses, short temper, and lack of interest in life in general. It felt every day like my life was about to be over. Tomorrow—no, the next day; and on and on it went.

Finally the news broke: an article on the front page of the local paper announced the big event. "Pilgrims Pride Coming Out of Bankruptcy," or some sort of startling headline. What would it say?

My mind raced—the phone rang. A close friend asked, "Have you read the paper today?"

"Not yet," I answered, "but I just saw the headline about Pilgrims. Have you read it?" I asked him.

"Good news, Brother," he blurted. "The article says that every vendor for Pilgrims is going to get one hundred percent of their money back!"

"What?" I couldn't believe it. Even though it was exactly what I had prayed for. "You're kidding, right? Don't kid about this."

"I'm not," he assured me, "that's what it said. I've watched these things all my life; this has never happened before. It's a first in America."

Never before had a billion-dollar American company come out of bankruptcy and paid every vendor all of their money back. I bowed my head and thanked my Father.

But God wasn't through.

That $100,000 that was originally over a year past due was now over two and a half years past due, but it wasn't even questioned. It was included in the total when the check finally came.

In fact, I was very confused when the check finally arrived and didn't match the $210,000 total I was looking for. It was for $223,000. They paid me interest. Is God good, or what?

So when you're down and feel there's no way out, remember this: God will make a way. If he needs to, He'll bankrupt a billion-

175

dollar corporation, reimburse all the vendors the full amount—
including bills over a year old, plus He'll pay them interest.

Lord, You are able. I am humbled. Use me however You wish.
I'm Yours. Forever. In Jesus's name, amen.

Dreams

Does God Still Use Dreams?

"But that night God came to Abimelech in a *dream* and told him, 'You are a dead man, for that woman you have taken is already married!'"

Genesis 20:3 (NLT)

My answer to this question used to be no, pure and simple. What would yours be? Are you sure?

Red Skelton (a comedian in the 1970s with his own prime-time show) used to have a recurring skit where he said to a guest, "Only fools are positive."

The guest would say, "Are you sure about that?"

Red would say, "I'm positive." Funny and ironic. We are often quite positive about something that we shouldn't be.

With that possibility in mind—since we are all mistaken at times—let's look at the biblical evidence of God's use of dreams.

In the Genesis 20 passage above, Abimelech had an entire conversation with God in his dream. God informed him that he was a dead man because Sarah was married. Abimelech responded in the dream by defending himself, saying he hadn't even touched her. God informed him that He had orchestrated that—not Abimelech. Then he commanded Abimelech to return Sarah to Abraham, threatening him with death if he didn't. Additionally, God told Abimelech that Abraham was a prophet. We often think of Abraham as the father of faith, but we don't usually include the detail of his being a prophet.

Notice that Abimelech didn't get up in the morning and say, "I had too much pizza last night! That was a weird dream I had."

177

No, he remembered and believed it as true and real. Perhaps there are times we should do the same.

In Genesis 28:12 Jacob dreamed of a stairway to heaven with angels going up and down it.

Notice that he didn't wake up in the morning and dismiss it. He set up a monument so the spot could be remembered and the story retold to all his descendants.

Jacob also had a dream that made him rich. God revealed what color the next generations of goats would be so Jacob could name those as his own—before they were born (Genesis 31:10-12).

Notice that he didn't wake up and ignore it; he acted on it by telling Laban which baby goats he would be willing to take.

When Jacob left Laban with his wives (Laban's two daughters), Laban chased them down to retrieve his idol. When he was about to overtake Jacob's caravan, God told him in a dream to leave Jacob alone (Genesis 31:24).

Notice that Joseph's dreams made his brothers quite mad (Genesis 37:5-11). Why would it bother them if dreams were just something silly to be dismissed? It bothered them because they were fully aware that dreams had important meanings.

In Genesis 40 and 41 Joseph interpreted the dreams of the Pharaoh's butler and baker, and both interpretations came true—literally. Did that only happen then? Keep reading.

Notice that Joseph fully expected the dreams to tell the future, and even asked the butler to remember him later. If he didn't totally trust the dreams, he would not have asked them both to remember him.

Gideon's great victory over Median was predicted (and believed) in a dream (Judges 7:13-15), after he was down to just three hundred men.

Notice that after the dream, Gideon fully expected victory and was no longer afraid to move forward with God's directions.

God visited Solomon in a dream after he replaced David as king to ask him what gift he would like (1 Kings 3:5). Solomon asked for wisdom—in the dream. Again, they had a whole conversation, and Solomon got exactly what God said—in the dream—that He would give him.

Notice that he wasn't surprised to receive what God promised him in the dream.

Job believed that God spoke in dreams:

> "He speaks in a *dream* or a vision of the night when people are in a deep sleep, lying on their beds."
>
> Job 33:15 (NCV)

Psalm 105:19 reveals that dreams are a way for God to reveal the future and His timing for it.

Proverbs 13:19 teaches that it's foolish not to believe and aspire to dreams. This was a quite interesting revelation to me, and once I read this I began to notice some things that I hadn't noticed before. Joseph's dreams inspired him through many years of difficulty; they help him through hard times. Gideon's dreams gave him confidence to move forward into battle though the odds were impossible. He knew victory was assured by God. I thought about these cases and others, and it dawned on me how glimpses of the future are motivators for believers. (That's also why I wrote *My Search for the Real Heaven*.)

In Daniel 1:17 God gave Daniel the ability to interpret dreams—proving that dreams have real-world meanings.

King Nebuchadnezzar's dream in Daniel 2 revealed a multitude of absolutely truthful details of the future. In fact, verse 29 announced that every minute detail of that prediction was absolutely certain. King Nebby's dream in Daniel 4 revealed a fact about his own future: if he didn't submit to God, he would live like an animal for seven years. It happened.

> *Lord, I praise You for Your personal, ongoing involvement in the lives of all these Old Testament characters. Open my eyes to what I need to see and understand about this. In Jesus's name, amen.*

New Testament Dreams

"When it was time to leave, they returned to their own
country by another route, for God had warned them in a
dream not to return to Herod."

Matthew 2:12 (NLT)

If you're inclined to think this only happened in the Old
Testament, think again. It's rampant.

In Matthew 1:20-21 God used a dream to communicate a
very important instruction to Joseph: you need to marry Mary!

Notice that Joseph didn't wake up from that dream and say,
"Wow, that was a wild dream. I dreamed I was supposed to go
ahead and marry Mary—even though she has obviously been
unfaithful! Dreams are one thing; reality is another. I know God
wants me to remain pure and avoid even the appearance of evil,
so I know I need to call off this marriage. Besides, if I don't, people will see that as an admission that I am actually the father!"
No, he simply obeyed. He completely changed his plans based
on a dream.

Additionally, God told him in a dream (Matthew 2:13) to flee
to Egypt to save the child's life. And then to return (Matthew
2:19) when Herod was dead and the threat was over. Each time
Joseph obeyed. What faith!

The wise men were warned in a dream (Matthew 2:12) not to
return to Herod.

There is one more Old Testament verse about dreams from
one of God's prophets: Joel. And it's interesting to note that Joel's
revelation on dreams is important enough to be quoted in the
first gospel sermon in Acts 2. Notice this quote:

"After this, I will pour my Spirit on everyone. Your sons
and daughters will prophesy. Your old men will dream

dreams. Your young men will see visions. In those days I will pour my Spirit on servants, on both men and women."

Joel 2:28-29 (GWT)

After what? Let's see what Peter said about that in Acts 2 when he quoted it in the first ever sermon. Notice what it was in context with:

"Then Peter stepped forward with the eleven other apostles and shouted to the crowd, 'Listen carefully, all of you, fellow Jews and residents of Jerusalem! Make no mistake about this. These people are not drunk, as some of you are assuming. Nine o'clock in the morning is much too early for that. No, what you see was predicted long ago by the prophet Joel: "In the last days," God says, "I will pour out my Spirit upon all people. Your sons and daughters will prophesy. Your young men will see visions, and your old men will dream dreams. In those days I will pour out my Spirit even on my servants—men and women alike—and they will prophesy.""

Acts 2:14-18 (NLT)

Although the local populace thought these strange people were simply drunk, Peter informed them that it was the real, actual, literal fulfillment of an ancient prophecy of Joel. This seems to usher in the possibility that God wasn't through with dreams; He still planned to use them.

My back-up theory on dreams was that perhaps God did use them in the New Testament, but just for a while—not anymore.

New Testament dreams that seemed to fit this theory were numerous. Paul was warned in a dream or vision (Acts 16:6-8) not to go into Asia. Immediately following this, he had one from a man in Macedonia pleading for help (Acts 16:9-10). This led them to conclude that God wanted them in Macedonia. There's never even a hint that they doubted these communications.

Cornelius (a Gentile) was granted a dream of vision that led him to send for Peter (Acts 10:1-8).

Meanwhile, Peter was told in a daytime dream that he was to accept the Gentiles into the kingdom (Acts 10:9-17).

Then God made sure they connected the dots between the two events (Acts 10:19-20).

This list could go on and on, but perhaps those will encourage you to study others on your own.

Lord, I never realized how often in the Bible You used dreams to communicate important things. If you are willing to share with me in this same manner, Lord, I'm open to it. Please help me recognize it. I am at Your service. In Jesus's name, amen.

One More Thing on Dreams and Visions

"In the same way, these people—who *claim authority* from their dreams—live immoral lives, defy authority, and scoff at supernatural beings."

Jude 1:8 (NLT)

But there's one other important and interesting fact about dreams in the Bible, and the enemy exploits this (in my opinion) on a regular basis. Let me explain.

There is definitely a big potential problem with dreams that I need to mention here: People can misuse them, misinterpret them, or invent them. Think a moment about these three issues.

Lord, please give me a deeper understanding of dreams. Help me never to assign significance to a dream that isn't there, and help me never to ignore a dream with an important message for me. Grant me wisdom and understanding and discernment in this area of my life. In Jesus's name, amen.

Misusing Dreams

"Interpreters of dreams pronounce *falsehoods* that give no comfort."

Zechariah 10:2 (NLT)

You can have a dream from God and disobey it. That would be one form of misuse. You can have a dream from God and doubt it. That is perhaps a more subtle form of misuse. God isn't in the habit of violating our consciences with things that we personally don't believe can happen, right?

If you were God, and you gave someone an important message in a dream but they never chose to believe it was from you or act on it, would you keep giving that person more communicative dreams? No.

I think this is similar to what Jesus faced when he said he couldn't do many miracles in that place because of their unbelief (Matthew 13:58).

Lord, help me to always obey Your instructions—no matter how You communicate them to me. In Jesus's name, amen.

Misinterpreting Dreams

"Do not listen to your *false prophets*, fortune-tellers, interpreters of *dreams*, mediums, and sorcerers who say, "The king of Babylon will not conquer you.'"

Jeremiah 27:9 (NLT)

False prophets were claiming that their dreams revealed safety from Babylon. Jeremiah's dreams contradicted. These men were doing this to gain favor and favors from the king. They were saying what they knew the king wanted to hear. While they didn't have the advantage of checking Scripture, we do.

Dreams will never contradict the Scriptures.

183

Lord, please don't let me believe something from a dream that contradicts Your Holy Word. In Jesus's name, amen.

Dream Inventing

"A hungry person *dreams of eating* but wakes up still hungry. A thirsty person dreams of drinking but is still faint from thirst when morning comes."

Isaiah 29:8 (NLT)

This may seem like a silly example, but it makes the point: be real. You may get a message from God in a dream some day, but it won't contradict reality. You can't have a healthy body by only eating in your dreams. Just sayin'.

Lord, help me to understand it if You're trying to tell me something. In Jesus's name, amen.

The Fate of Those Who Invent Dreams or Control Others with Dreams

God had some very specific instructions on how to handle false prophets; people who invent dreams and promote interpretations of them that are for their own benefit. False prophets were to be stoned. Pure and simple:

"Suppose there are prophets among you or those who dream dreams about the future, and they promise you signs or miracles. The false prophets or visionaries who try to lead you astray *must be put to death*."

Deuteronomy 13:1, 5

Think of it this way: I couldn't come to town and say, "Hi, I'm prophet Steve. I had a dream that brought me here today. Your city here is so evil that if everyone doesn't repent by next Tuesday at 2:00 p.m., God will send fire from heaven to destroy you."

Next Tuesday at 2:01 p.m., and nothing has happened. What do you do? You have a rock in your hand and you're looking for me. Why? Because I'm a false prophet.

Notice that the one defense I absolutely could not use (biblically) is this: "Oh it happened in the unseen—you just don't know it yet. You are already dead. I'm a spiritual man and you aren't, and I have seen it in the spiritual realm."

Not. Stone me.

Now think about it. What is this really teaching about biblical prophecy? That it's literal. But that's a book for another day.

Lord, I confess that I need spiritual wisdom and discernment. In Jesus's name, amen.

Tracey's Dream

"But **her baby died** during the night when she rolled over on it."

1 Kings 3:19 (NLT)

Tracey had a daughter who passed away from SIDS. She felt so torn. Part of her wanted to be with her in heaven, and part wanted to stay with her husband and son here on earth. She muddled through each day like a zombie, barely able to function. Even simple tasks like taking showers were a struggle. She ate little and slept fitfully. It felt like her world had come apart at the seams. Until the dream.

Finally, she had a dream that changed everything. She dreamed of an older man. He appeared, and she immediately felt at peace with him though she didn't recognize him; they had never met. They were standing in a very bright place. The brightness didn't hurt her eyes, but it was brighter than she had ever seen or imagined brightness could be. It seemed to permeate every molecule of everything it touched. And it touched everything.

Then she noticed the music. Music filled that place like water in a glass; nothing was left untouched by it. It wasn't a recognizable instrument, but the sounds it made were phenomenal. Amazing.

Without really thinking, Tracey asked if Kristen was warm— a strange question, and the gentle man chuckled. He said that she was warm and beautiful.

Tracey said, "Right away I loved this man."

"Everyone up here loves her so much," the man continued.

That too gave Tracey comfort.

Then Tracey asked, "Can I go and see Kristen and then come back?"

"No," the kind man said with a touch of sadness in his eyes, "that won't be possible."

"But I can leave my husband, Jerry, and our son, Josh, and go be with Kristen," Tracey heard herself saying, because she wanted so badly to see her.

"That's true, you can," he replied. Then he leaned over and whispered, "Kristen is doing really well here, and she is loved so much. Why don't you stay with Josh and Jerry for now, and come back when you are supposed to."

The instant Tracey agreed, he was gone.

"The next thing I knew," Tracey said, "I was sitting straight up in my bed with a vivid recollection of the whole dream. My heart was pounding as I stared into the total darkness of our bedroom in the middle of the night. I truly believe that heaven will so exceed anyone's expectations we will all be in awe."

Lord, thank You for Tracey's dream and for the comfort it gave her to get a glimpse of heaven. Bless her through the pain and adjustment of having lost a child. Comfort her with the memory of this dream on the days she misses her most. Use her and this experience to encourage many others. In Jesus's name, amen.

Stephanie's Dream

"How I wish today that you of all people would understand the way to peace. *But now it is too late, and peace is
hidden from your* eyes."

Luke 19:42 (NLT)

I was speaking in Texas. The youth minister's wife, Stephanie,
said she wanted to talk before I left the church building that
night. "Sure," I said, and we sat down in the preacher's office.
"What's on your mind?"

"When I was a six-year-old playing soccer, they diagnosed
me with a heart murmur but said lots of people have them and
it probably wouldn't cause any issues. But when I was co-captain
of the cheerleading squad as a senior in high school at the top
of a pyramid at the homecoming game, high in the air, I passed
out and fell all the way to the asphalt track around the football
field. They rushed me to the hospital. A valve in my heart had
ceased to function, and if I hadn't been young and fit, I would
have died on the spot. They did emergency valve replacement the
old-fashioned way: open heart surgery. My heart had doubled in
size, and they couldn't believe it hadn't exploded. I came through
fine, finished my stay in recovery, and even ate a meal before my
grandparents left to return to their home on the other side of
Texas. I remember sitting in bed and picking up my fork to eat
again—then nothing. I blacked out. The heart had stopped.

"The nurses sounded the 'Code Blue' alarm, and a team of
experts rushed to my room—including my doctor. I had flat-lined.
They shocked me with the defibrillator three times. Nothing.
Since I had just gone through open heart surgery, they couldn't
just press on my chest to get it pumping again, so the doctor tore
my rib cage open and began messaging my heart directly with his
hands, willing it to beat again. It's called open cardiac massage.
Nothing. Fifteen minutes. Nothing. Thirty minutes. Nothing.
Forty minutes. Nothing. Everyone but him gave up. He pumped

187

and squeezed it, frantic to save my life. Then at forty-five minutes a wavy line began to appear on the screen. But just as hope returned—I slipped into a coma. For three and a half weeks.

"Now let me tell you what I saw while I was there.

"I was in a room with a great brightness. Someone was standing across from me. I suddenly realized it was an angel. He had on a white robe with blue tassels that hung down the sides. He had long brown hair and massive wings. He also had a golden trumpet and a very deep voice. When he spoke it sounded like thunder, but it was very calming in spite of that. I was overwhelmed and could not speak at first.

"The angel said, 'Don't be afraid. It's not your time; you must go back.' Then he added, 'You must get your life in order.' He comforted me with his massive embrace, wings and all. It made me feel like warm oil was running through my whole body, soothing and relaxing and peaceful.

"I knew I needed to get my life straight. At the time I had been doing things I shouldn't have and hanging out with people that weren't the greatest influence. I had a deep desire to get my life right—before it was too late."

Lord, thank You for the second chances you give people each and every day. Help us to take advantage of it before it's eternally too late. In Jesus's name, amen.

Panta's Dream

"When the Lord brought back his exiles to Jerusalem, it was like a ***dream!***"

Psalm 126:1 (NLT)

One Sunday morning many years ago, we had a response at the end of a sermon by a mother and her son. They were from Thailand, and I'd never seen them before. They wanted to be baptized.

Days later, I found out who they were. They were Buddhist, and as a result of her response to the gospel of Jesus Christ, her husband had moved out, leaving her and the boy alone. This is common in the Buddhist culture, but a shock to me.

Not long after that, I was able to meet Panta and her son, and I asked her what led to her conversion, especially in light of the huge personal cost for doing so. This was her response:

"I grew up in Thailand, the youngest of two daughters. Our father became a Buddhist monk; Buddhism was my inherited religion. My older sister, Tiew, met her American husband in 1975 while he was serving in the US Army, assigned to Thailand. They married, and when they left for the US, I thought I would never see her again. We were two years apart and very close. I will never forget the sadness of saying good-bye at the airport.

"As Tiew was growing up, she had become dissatisfied with the Buddhist beliefs. She desperately searched for better spiritual answers than Buddhism had to offer. Before she left, Dad gave her an English book about Buddhism, explaining that he didn't want her to be forced to become a Christian. Not long after leaving for the US, she wrote to us that she had become a Christian, upsetting us all, but especially Dad.

"When Mom was dying in 1978, Tiew returned for a visit. Dad was very upset with Tiew's conversion, but she was undeterred and shared her faith with me. She invited me to go to church services with her there, and I went out of respect for her. It was just a way to get to spend time with my sister during the short visit. Mom died soon after the visit.

"She returned six years later, in 1984, this time with a nine-month-old son, Andrew. Grandchildren tend to put a smile on a grandfather's face, in spite of their differences. Again, Tiew shared her life of faith with me, and we studied the Bible together. And again, I went to church services with her. She was very committed.

"One year later I was married with my own baby boy. It was a huge surprise when Tiew contacted me to report that my VISA had been approved. Additionally, my husband, Warut, and my son, Tong, would be able to join me if I accepted. When we arrived in February of 1986, Tiew also had a baby girl, Amy. We lived happily with them for the first few years.

"Tiew continued to study the Bible with me and invite me to church with them, and I went some. Warut got a job, and we eventually got a place of our own. Warut was transferred, so we lived a great distance from Tiew, but we always got together for the Christmas holidays. No matter where we were when we were together, Tiew and Bobby always went to church and invited us to accompany them.

"Finally, Tiew came to our area on a business trip and was able to spend a couple of days with me and my family. That Saturday night before going to bed, I asked what she wanted to do the next day, since it was her birthday. She responded that she wanted me to go to church with her and then return to that church without her the following Sunday, although she would be gone. I reluctantly agreed, a strange birthday gift for my sister.

"We went together on her birthday, and I knew I'd made a promise to go the next Sunday by myself.

"Saturday night came, and I was very troubled. I knew I had promised my sister, but I felt it was something for Americans, not Thai people. That night I sat in bed and prayed, '*If You're there, God, and You truly are the highest God of gods, then You're going to need to help me. I'm confused and not sure of what I need to do.*'

"I fell asleep that night and had one of the most life-changing dreams. I dreamed I was standing on a glass platform, suspended in the air. Above were clouds and a bright sky, and below was nothing but darkness.

"I heard a voice saying, 'Panta, do you believe in God?'

"I was speechless. I didn't know how to answer. I had always worshipped Buddha.

"Again, the voice asked, 'Do you believe in God?'

"The platform started to break into tiny pieces, and I found myself about to fall toward the darkness below.

"Before falling, however, my sister's hands from the sky grabbed me, saving me.

"I knew the dream was from God, and I knew I had to go back to that church.

"Some of the members there recognized me from the times I had visited there with my sister. They offered a Bible study, and within weeks I called Tiew and told her that my son and I wanted to be baptized and that I wanted her husband, Bobby, to baptize us. She and her entire family quickly flew in. Bobby baptized us, and as their daughter watched the event, she decided she wanted it too, so Bobby baptized all three of us.

"God's love is so amazing. His mercy is indescribable. Just as He listened to Tiew's prayer of desperation when she was nineteen years old, asking Him to show her the way, He listened to mine. Since He answered both of our prayers back then, many more have been answered in so many special ways. Because of God's love, Tiew never gave up on me. Because of God's love, my son has touched many lives, young and old. Because of God's love, I am joyful to have the confidence in knowing that my sister will always be by my side spiritually through all eternity."

Lord, thank you for stories like Panta's, that have helped me to realize that You can still use dreams to communicate important messages anytime You wish. Thank You for the reminder that You aren't called, "The Great I WAS," or "The Great I USED to Be," but, "The Great I AM." In Jesus's name, amen.

Marie's Dream

"During the night God spoke to him in a vision."

Genesis 46:2 (NLT)

Marie did not have a good relationship with her mother. Her mother was verbally abusive on a daily basis, very manipulative in their relationship, and constantly belittling Marie in every way possible. Marie had no respect for her as a person because of the daily mental abuse she suffered at her mom's hands.

Marie's mom did not have God in her life either. She had no relationship at all with Jesus. Self-admittedly, she wasn't a God-loving person.

When her mother died, Marie was relieved. She felt a little guilty for not being sad, but the absence of the abusive relationship helped her to relax, for the first time in years. The more time passed, the better Marie felt. This was amplified by friendly counsel from Marie's father-in-law, who had been in a similar situation with his own mother many years before.

Then the dream.

Marie saw her mother returning to her. It was like a flicker of light, and her mom was back. Ill feelings rose up inside Marie —until she realized her mother couldn't even look at her, like embarrassment prevented it. It took Marie a moment to realize what prevented her mom from looking her way. It was the brightness that surrounded, even permeated, every ounce of Marie's being. The brightness had its source in Jesus. Marie realized in that moment that she was worth more—much more—than her mother had ever realized or admitted. It gave Marie an inner peace and joy and contentment that was beyond words. Marie saw God's love leaking out of her onto others, and the happiness she felt was overwhelming. The whole scene reinforced Marie's self-worth beyond measure.

Marie awoke and still remembers every detail of this comforting scene.

Lord, thank You for being the great "I AM," instead of the "I Was," or the "I Used to Be." And thank You for reminding me that You can still do anything You choose: miracles, visions, dreams, etc. In Jesus's name, amen.

Julie's Dream

"I see a *terrifying vision*: I see the betrayer betraying, the
destroyer destroying."

Isaiah 21:2 (NLT)

Recently I went down to the dealership for an oil change. It's a
nice place with a Christian owner, and I like to do business with
believers whenever possible.

As I arrived in the service area and checked my car in with
the girl holding a clipboard, there was a short delay before we
could finish the paperwork. While we waited, she said, "What
do you do?"

"Well," I began, "I'm sort of an accidental author."

That usually gets funny looks, because it's rare to even meet an
author, much less one who became one, "accidentally."

"How did that happen?" she replied.

I told her the story about finding the envelope from my dad
after his death and that the envelope was sealed with a note on
the front saying, "If I'm no longer living and this is still unopened,
destroy it without opening." (The whole story is in *My Search for
the Real Heaven*, if you're interested.)

Then I told her I was writing a new book on spiritual warfare.
That always seems to peak people's interest.

"Well, I've got a story for you on that subject," she exclaimed.

"Tell me," I urged.

"Well," she said, "I was on drugs and a dealer. And God gave
me a dream one day that caused me to become a Christian."

My interested skyrocketed. "What did you see in the dream?"
I promptly asked.

"He showed me what it was like to go to hell," she stated flatly.
"Once I saw that, I was done with drugs. Never used again, and I
have no desire to. I belong to God now."

"Wow." That's all I could think to say.

Lord, thank You for having the ability and the power to turn a drug dealer with no hope into a powerful Christian witness for Your kingdom. Use me to reach others like you're using her. In Jesus's name, amen.

Joe Nichols's Dream

"And anyone whose name was not found recorded in the Book of Life was thrown into the *lake of fire*."

Revelation 20:15 (NLT)

In 2004 a country song by Joe Nichols caught me by surprise. It took my breath away. Although the music is much more compelling than just reading the words, I include the words to that song about a dream here. I never found out if someone really had this dream, or if it's just a good song, but it's heart wrenching, to say the least. Please read it slowly, letting the words soak in as you experience the scenes he describes. Try to imagine the hopelessness the singer feels as he tells you his dream.

"Revelation"
by Joe Nichols

Somewhere in Vietnam a nineteen-year-old soldier stumbled from a bar room; he said I must be seeing things, that bourbon hit me like a baseball bat.

In Belfast, Ireland a little lady dropped her shovel in her garden. As she raced across her yard to ask her neighbor Mrs. Clancy, "What was that?"

In Memphis, Tennessee a teacher raised the window closest to the river, and the children in her classroom swore they heard a choir singing down the street.

In Washington, DC, a private secretary's lips began to
quiver, and the president just put aside some papers and
rose quickly to his feet.

I lay in a cheap motel in the arms of someone else's
woman when a loud explosion rocked the room and
turned the morning into night. I jumped out of bed and
ran into the street with hardly any clothes on, and as the
sky lit up, my heart stood still, and I could feel my face
turn white.

All at once the clouds rolled back, and there stood Jesus
Christ in all his glory, and I realized the saddest eyes I'd
ever seen were looking straight at me.

I guess I was awakened by the penetrating sound of my
own screaming—it didn't take me long to stumble out of
bed and fall down on my knees as tears rolled down my
face I cried "Dear God, I'm thankful I was only dreaming.
If I never go to hell, Lord, it's because you scared it out
of me."

Words like these that spur emotions like mine right now com-
pel me to want to do anything God requires to avoid this scene.
How about you?

*Lord, please scare every bit of the hell out of me, too. Help me
not to be blind to my own faults and weaknesses. Open my eyes
to anything that separates me from You so I can correct it right
away because I know You could arrive any day now, and I
want to be ready for that moment. In Jesus's name, amen.*

The Lonely Rock Climber

"Your Majesty, this is the dream's meaning: It is the sen-
tence of the Most High, delivered to my master the king.
You will be driven away from other humans and will live
with the wild animals. You will eat grass like cattle and will

be washed by dew from heaven. Seven periods of time will pass over you, until you acknowledge that the Most High dominates human kingship, giving it to anyone he wants. And when he said to leave the deepest root of the tree—that means your kingship will again be yours, once you acknowledge that heaven rules all. Therefore, Your Majesty, *please* accept my advice: *remove your sins* by doing what is right; remove your wrongdoing by showing mercy to the poor. Then your safety will be long lasting."

Daniel 4:24-27 (CEB)

One area is worth emphasizing concerning dreams. Just like in Julie's case, dreams might sometimes be used by God (on you) on occasion to wake you up to our own sins. Most of us are quite blind in this area. We don't really understand how important it is to remove certain things from our lives because we're so used to them being there; we're comfortable, in spite of the fact that we know deep down we should refrain from them. You know what I'm talking about. Let me illustrate how important it is to cut something out of our life—something that could keep you out of heaven.

A few years ago, a lone mountain climber slipped and fell in a crevasse. His arm got lodged, and he hung there for days.

Ultimately his arm was dead from lack of blood flow. He was out of water, so he drank his own urine. When your life is threatened, you can do things you normally couldn't do. He began to realize that if he didn't take drastic steps, he was going to die right there, and soon. All he had to work with was a small, dull pocketknife. So he cut his arm off with it—in order to live PHYSICALLY.

Christians are people who realize the hopelessness of their desperate situation and have made the decision to cut the things out of their life that will keep them from living forever. They cut out things that lead to SPIRITUAL death so they can have eternal life with God.

Is there something you need to cut out that might keep you from heaven? My guess is that the answer to this is yes. You have to cut something out of your life to go to heaven. What is it? Cut it out.

Lord, give me the courage to do what I have to to make it to heaven with You—no matter what it is. In Jesus's name, amen.

My Dream

"For the word of God is alive and powerful. It is sharper than the sharpest two-edged *sword*, cutting between soul and spirit, between joint and marrow. It exposes our innermost thoughts and desires."

Hebrews 4:12 (NLT)

I dream but usually don't remember the details. One morning I awoke, and that wasn't the case.

I lay in bed thinking about what I had just seen. "Lord," I prayed, "if I'm supposed to learn something from this dream, please help me to know what it is and correctly apply it."

I was concealed in the woods with tall grass and prickly bushes all around me. I knew an enemy was close, and I was trying to remain ready, focused, alert. I had a weapon but couldn't really tell what it was. Scripture calls the Bible the "Sword of the Spirit," and maybe that's what it was.

My eyes darted back and forth quickly, watching the landscape for any flicker of movement. I knew the enemy was close, very close.

I felt the onset of fear—like a great battle was about to begin, but the outcome was certain. I was destined to win. I knew it in my heart; knew it like I knew my name. I was sure, certain, confident. Not arrogant or uppity, just peaceful that it would work out, like when you've read a book, know the ending, and you're rereading it to enjoy the journey again.

Then I realized it—I knew what I was supposed to take from this setting.

Faith is our camouflage. When we rest in the stillness of faith, the enemy can't see us to hurt us. But if we let fear become our focus, we begin to tremble, revealing our position to the enemy. Remember, this is war.

> "Stay alert! *Watch out for your great enemy, the devil.* He prowls around like a roaring lion, looking for someone to devour."
>
> 1 Peter 5:8 (NLT)

Lord, help me to rest in peace and stillness, knowing You are in control, You are the King, and You have adopted me into Your family. Thank You for protecting me from the enemy. Show me what to do for the Kingdom today. In Jesus's name, amen.

Preparing for Battle

God's Friends

"Abraham believed God, and God counted him as righteous because of his faith. He was even called the *friend of God*."

James 2:23 (NLT)

Noah was a friend of God. So God shared his plans to flood the earth. You share your plans with your close friends, right?

David, Moses, Joseph, and Job—all friends of God. Close friends have an intimate relationship. There's daily, ongoing, conversational relationship between God and His friends. That's what friends do. They talk. Long and often.

Abraham was a friend of God. That's why God told him what He planned to do with Sodom and Gomorrah. You always let your friends know what you're planning, right? That's also why Abraham felt comfortable discussing the possibility of holding off if there were some righteous people living there. You give feedback based on your opinions to your friends, right?

Notice also that at the end of his ministry, Jesus told his disciples:

> "I no longer call you slaves, because a master doesn't confide in his slaves. *Now you are my friends*, since I have told you everything the Father told me."
>
> John 15:15 (NLT)

Are you a friend of God?

Lord, I want to be Your friend. Help me to spend more time in Your word and in prayer. Help me to know Your ways better,

199

*and help me to be more like Jesus every day. In Jesus's name,
amen.*

Commitment

"They are all skilled swordsmen, experienced warriors.
Each wears a sword on his thigh, **ready to defend the king
against an attack** in the night."

Song of Solomon 3:8 (NLT)

I read an account written by a true warrior, a Navy Seal. After
serving several tours in Iraq during the Gulf War, he was assigned
for a time to help with a study on blood pressure and how combat affects it. He had been in several heated firefights near the
end of his final tour, and a couple of his comrades were killed
by sniper fire. Following the deaths of these close friends he had
some panic attacks and some severe blood pressure problems.
They thought he was ideal to help them discover tendencies and
remedies for future soldiers.

He was put in a simulator and first experienced normal daily
activities. Then his group on patrol was ambushed by the enemy.
Prior to the attack his blood pressure was high. But, to the surprise of the medical staff, once the battle began his blood pressure
actually went down. It was below normal. Does this puzzle you?
Here's what happened:

He had been through extensive training for many years. And
then he had literally been in thousands of combat situations. His
training had been so thorough that once the battle began his
training kicked in and he actually relaxed, causing his blood pressure to go down instead of up (like it would have done for me).

In other words, he was so prepared to be a warrior that his
blood pressure was a problem before the battle, but not after; his
body actually relaxed and went on auto-pilot once what he was
trained for finally began.

That's how Christians should be in the daily battle for the kingdom that we face. We should be a) well-prepared through Bible study and prayer, b) expecting an attack from the enemy (Satan and his forces), and c) efficient and effective once the fighting starts.

Are you ready?

> *Lord, help me to be totally prepared for the big battles in life that I must face. I want You to be proud of me once the fighting starts. I want to bring great glory to Your Name. Show me where I'm weak and need additional training, and then please provide the people and the resources I need to remedy those issues. In Jesus's name, amen.*

Deeper Roots

"And you who are left in Judah, who have escaped the ravages of the siege, will *put roots down in your own soil* and will *grow up and flourish.*"

2 Kings 19:30 (NLT)

There was once a drought in a small community with apple orchards. Apples were the main source of income for the families there, so the lack of rain was bound to have a big economic impact.

But one farmer's trees looked better than everyone else's, so the others asked him what he was doing differently. They discovered his secret.

"Nothing, right now," was his reply. "But when these trees were very young, I deliberately deprived them of water. This made their roots grow much deeper—deep enough to survive and flourish through a severe drought."

God often works like that. The difficulties we face on a regular basis make us turn to Him.

Delaying the answer to a prayer can often have a good long-term effect. We realize our dependence on Him, and spend more time in prayer and Bible study. So if your prayer answers don't come as quickly and perfectly as you hope, remember:

He is at work in the details of your life. He is the Potter. Be that soft clay in His hands, and wait on Him. He's worth the wait.

Lord, forgive me for my impatience. Help me to learn Your ways and trust Your provision. In Jesus's name, amen.

Learn to Pray

"Once Jesus was in a certain place praying. As he finished, one of his disciples came to him and said, '**Lord, teach us to pray**, just as John taught his disciples.'"

LUKE 11:1 (NLT)

Just as it became clear to the disciples, I hope by now it's clear to you: the battle between the kingdom of light and the kingdom of darkness is fought through prayer. When we pray in the seen, things happen in the unseen. It's as if God is waiting for you to ask for the things He's already poised to do; like He's decided not to do what you're not ready to help Him with. So, help Him!

Satan's plans against us are thwarted through prayer.

Disease and pain are affected by prayer.

Death is delayed through prayer. And if you don't believe that, ask Hezekiah (the king who prayed to live and was granted 15 more years) about it when you see him in heaven!

Prayer in the seen literally affects the events in the unseen and the plans of the King.

Satan wants you to neglect prayer and doubt it's power BECAUSE it's so powerful. It's a deception thing, see? That way you're easier to conquer. It's a tactic.

Finally, notice that the disciples never asked Jesus to teach them to preach, or even to do miracles. They asked Him to teach them to pray because they understood that connection between prayer and true power. It's real.

Lord, I want to truly learn how to pray with power. Give me understanding and wisdom and insight. Grant me courage to ask for what's best overall rather than what I want right now. Forgive me for sometimes treating You in the past as a "Santa in the sky," Lord, and help me to have the discernment I need to ask for what's most important in Your overall scheme and plan. In Jesus's name, amen.

Clean the Person

"If you *declare with your mouth, 'Jesus is Lord,' and if you believe in your heart* that God raised Jesus from the dead, you will be saved. We believe with our hearts, and so we are made right with God. And we declare with our mouths that we believe, and so we are saved. As the Scripture says, "Anyone who trusts in him will never be disappointed."

Romans 10:9-11

But wait, don't the demons believe? Yes:

"You believe that there is one God. You do well. *Even the demons believe*—and tremble!"

James 2:19 (NKJV)

James even says that faith alone; faith without works of obedience is dead, worthless, useless:

"*Faith*, if it does not have works (deeds and actions of obedience to back it up), **by itself is** destitute of power (inoperative, *dead*)."

James 2:17 (AMP)

So how should I express my faith? In obedience, just like Peter explained in the first gospel sermon ever in Acts 2 when the Jews realized they had literally crucified the Son of God. They said, "What must we do?" not, "What must we believe?" or, "What must we say?"

"When the people heard this, they were deeply upset. They asked Peter and the other apostles, 'Brothers, what should we do?' Peter answered them, 'All of *you must turn to God and change the way you think and act*, and each of *you must be baptized* in the name of Jesus Christ *so that your sins will be forgiven*. Then you will receive the Holy Spirit as a gift.'"

Acts 2:37-38 (GWT)

So you see, first of all you must have faith. All else without faith is worthless. Baptism is worthless, just getting wet—without faith. But believer's baptism is done in faith, so it's just an act of obedience, like accepting a gift you could never earn, like taking hold a life preserver in the middle of a raging sea because it's the only thing that can save you at that moment. Accept Jesus, become a disciple, obey His commands, and then you can join the battle against the true enemy—the unseen ones. It's not a different religious group that's the enemy; it's Satan and his forces. His goal is to get us all fighting amongst ourselves. Sure, we can all learn something from each other; some can learn grace, some can learn about the Holy Spirit's ongoing activity in our lives, some can learn about prophecy or end times Bible verses that motivate others toward evangelism. Some can teach about heaven or prayer or love, but before you can battle the enemy you must make sure you have God on your side. If you haven't made a covenant with Him, you need to do that first. This also includes confessing your sins and submitting to Jesus as Lord and Savior and obeying the great commission (Matthew 28:18-20). David Platt covers this well in his book, "Radical."

All this "cleans the person." The person must be clean before he or she can clean the area and claim it for the kingdom.

Lord, I want to be in covenant with You so I can have access to Your help and Your strength. Then open my mind to see and remedy any unconfessed sin. I want to be as clean and white as snow in Your sight—just like Jesus. In Jesus's name, amen.

Clean the Area

Demons hate to be near people praising God, and they especially hate praise music! They can't stand it. They leave.

> "Whenever the tormenting spirit from God troubled Saul, *David would play the harp. Then Saul would feel better, and the tormenting spirit would go away.*"
>
> 1 Samuel 16:23 (NLT)

Praise is also called the "sacrifice" of praise, so I guess that to God it's in the same category as the other sacrifices He was offered:

> "Let us offer through Jesus a *continual sacrifice of praise* to God, proclaiming our allegiance to his name."
>
> Hebrews 13:15 (NLT)

Singing and praising God helped Paul find joy even in prison, and led to the conversion of the Philippian jailer in Acts:

> "Around midnight Paul and Silas were praying and singing hymns to God, and the other prisoners were listening. Suddenly, there was a massive earthquake, and the prison was shaken to its foundations. All the doors immediately flew open, and the chains of every prisoner fell off! The jailer woke up to see the prison doors wide open. He assumed the prisoners had escaped, so he drew his sword to kill himself. But Paul shouted to him, 'Stop! Don't kill yourself! We are all here!' The jailer called for lights and ran to the dungeon and fell down trembling before Paul and Silas. Then he brought them out and asked, 'Sirs, *what must I do to be saved?*' They replied, '*Believe in the Lord Jesus* and you will be saved, along with everyone in your household.' And they shared the word of the Lord with him and with all who lived in his household. Even at that hour of the night, the jailer cared for them and washed

their wounds. Then he *and everyone in his household were immediately baptized.*"

Acts 16:25-33 (NLT)

As it became known to friends and acquaintances that I was writing on the subject of spiritual warfare, I began to get more and more calls and requests for demonic-type issues in the lives of people. Some came from people I knew, who didn't feel comfortable sharing with others, and others came from total strangers. I got phone calls, emails, letters, and requests for help and advice from a variety of people from a smorgasbord of religious backgrounds. In my attempts to help and encourage these folks, some demonic connections became apparent and need to be shared here in this context.

You can't clean an area from the demonic without removing any connection to the demonic. These items can either be hidden, appear neutral, be forgotten, or be a gift from someone that looks harmless. They can include items from tribal people in Africa or South America, seemingly harmless things like Ouija boards or tarot cards, horoscopes, gifts, letters, photos, objects, movies, books, and many other things. You get the picture. Demons need a gateway to get into a persons life. Drugs, beer, wine, hidden secrets, and many other things can be included. It can even be things hidden on the house or property before it became yours, with no apparent connection to you. But their presence a) gives them an opening into your life, and b) gives them a beachhead to work from in attacking you. Ask God to show you what and where they are, and them remove them.

I have known some who chose to burn them. One man I know prayed, collected, and burned, repeating the process after each burning. He ended up burning items for days. Then his connection to the occult was severed. He renounced all evil in his life, even destroying R-rated movies. Once he finished, he never felt so free. Take your time; get it right, get it done: clean the area.

This must be done before you can claim the area for the kingdom of God.

Lord, I want the place where I live to be completely free from Satan's influence. In the Name of Jesus Christ, Messiah, I command that everything evil and everything connected to evil be revealed and expelled. I pledge allegiance to You and to the Lamb of God. Make this a safe haven for Your word, Your commands, Your people, and Your plans. In Jesus's name and by His power, amen.

Claim the Area for God

"*You have put pagan symbols on your doorposts* and behind your doors. *You have left me* and climbed into bed with these detestable gods."

Isaiah 57:8a (NLT)

"*Commit yourselves wholeheartedly to these words of mine.* Tie them to your hands and wear them on your forehead as reminders. Teach them to your children. Talk about them when you are at home and when you are on the road, when you are going to bed and when you are getting up. *Write them on the doorposts of your house and on your gates.*"

Deuteronomy 11:18-20 (NLT)

Once the land is free from any connection to evil, pray a wall around the property. Spread the stakes out wide. Dedicate the people and the property to the glory and expansion of God's eternal kingdom.

I have shared the "stake" story with some churches and some men's retreats over the last few years. The reaction has been something special. When I finish a men's retreat, for example, I always like to open it up for discussion, feedback, complaints, and takea-ways, things folks can actually take away and use in their daily lives. The responses have been quite encouraging—in spite of the "weird" feeling I would sometimes get from sharing this in an open discussion.

One elder said, "I'm going home to stake out my house, my farm, and our church."

A minister said, "This makes sense—we're at war, according to Ephesians 6, right?"

On another occasion I was leading a men's retreat for a church that was involved in a methamphetamine drug rehab program. When I asked for take aways at the end, one big guy raised his hand and stood to speak. He had tattoos running up and down his muscular arms and shoulders. "I'm from a small town in Oklahoma," he began, "and everyone in my town that I know of is on drugs. My brother committed suicide. My mother is think-ing about suicide. My mom and dad's only grandson is in jail for drugs…I'm going home and staking out the whole town. I'll drive out all four roads that lead to our city and put some big stakes out." He finished with tears streaming down his face. The whole group erupted with applause and stood, patting him on the back, offering words of encouragement.

It can't hurt, right?

Lord, forgive me for limiting your power of protection from evil in the past. Open my eyes, ears, heart, and mind to Your ways—no matter how silly it sounds, Lord. Help me to lean on Your promises of strength and protection as I face each new day. Use me for Your glory, and show me what to do today for the kingdom. In Jesus name, amen.

Prayer: Precision Tool of Dedicated Christians

Prayer is the Battle

"Elijah was as human as we are, and yet when he prayed earnestly that no rain would fall, none fell for three and a half years!"

James 5:17 (NLT)

As I'm sure you can tell by this point, the crux of spiritual warfare is centered on prayer. Your intimate, personal, daily, conversational relationship with the Father is the pivotal point for kingdom activity all around you. Are you willing to join the war? Or will you end up an unprepared victim of collateral damage? It's up to you. God gave you free will; a choice in this matter.

But for those willing to step forward and focus on what's eternally important, this is a conflict you don't want to miss—for a multitude of reasons (see the "Rewards" chapter in *My Search for the Real Heaven*).

So here are some final thoughts, words of encouragement, and prayer ideas that will change your life and your attitude—if you let them.

Lord, give us all a kingdom focus and a clear direction so we can make an eternal difference. In Jesus's name, amen.

A Few More Prayer Ideas

"Praise be to *God*, who *has not rejected my prayer* or withheld his love from me!"

Psalm 66:20 (NIV)

Throughout this book I have scattered a variety of prayers that I'm certain Satan hates. He hates all prayers. I found a verse one day that reveals Satan's native language:

"You belong to your father, *the devil*, and you want to carry out your father's desires. He was a murderer from the beginning, not holding to the truth, for there is no truth in him. *When he lies, he speaks his native language*, for he is a liar and the father of lies."

John 8:44 (NIV)

As I said before, these prayers aren't formulas that God has to respond to when you repeat the proper words; there are no automatic responses of the Almighty based on our reciting a magic formula or sequence of vowels and consonants. It's all about relationship. I hope my prayers have encouraged you, enlightened you, and, most of all, empowered you to a deeper and more constant state of personal prayer.

Years ago I noticed that I prayed more when things were bad, and less when things were going good. After that discovery I worked to make my prayer life more even, constant, and consistent. Even more than that, I have worked to train myself to react with prayer first rather than last, like I used to do. It has made all the difference in the world. I hope you can discover that same peace and joy.

I just couldn't end a book on spiritual warfare and prayer without including a few special ones I have prayed during the course of my life. Don't get me wrong, I'm still learning and creating new ones, and probably will until I die. I felt it was inappropriate, however, to close the cover on this subject (for now) without including these Bible-based prayers that have meant so much to me.

On more thing before I get to these final few. It's on the subject of depression.

As I revealed in the stories on the preceding pages, I have faced some massive "Giants" in the course of my life; especially my business life. Like any man, I focused too much on my career and the provision for my family, and too little on faith and how God delivers. So I have often panicked and worried when I felt "the end was near," so to speak. Potential bankruptcy stared me in the face more than once. I had been so vocal about my witness and my Christianity that I feared bankruptcy would bring great shame on my family and on my church. So far, that has never happened. But I finally realized that my real problem was pride, and that bringing shame on the church or the family was a way to hide behind the pride in a "religious" way. I kept repeating this cycle every time a new giant threatened to tear down my little kingdom. A friend taught me a little phrase that helped me relax and focus in spite of the threat. I guess it was sort of like David gathering his stones, focusing his eyes on his enemy, and then taking a deep breath before starting his windup. This silly little phrase might sound stupid and petty to you, but it helped me through; help me relax and turn the situation over to God. So I share it with you here and now, and pray it helps: "They can't kill me and eat me. It's illegal."

Lord, when it feels like the whole world is against me, remind me: they can't kill me and eat me; it's illegal. Remind me that You are in control, and that whatever I face won't be alone— You will be right there to help me. I trust Your provision. Forgive my lack of faith in the past. In Jesus's name, amen.

A King With a Foot Disease

"In the thirty-ninth year of his reign, *Asa developed a serious foot disease. Yet* even with the severity of his disease, *he did not seek the Lord's help but turned only to his physicians. So he died* in the forty-first year of his reign."

2 Chronicles 16:12-13

Wow. There's a startling statement for you. Asa only sought the help of the medical experts of the day. This offended God, so God let him die. Who made you? God. Who can fix you when you're broke? God. Ask Him for the help you need. He might say, "Yes," and He might not, but you never know until you ask. Ask for what you want. Then accept His answer and move forward.

Lord, when I'm sick or hurt, remind me that You are the one who can fix me. Forgive me for only seeking doctors and medicines in the past. In Jesus's name, amen.

On-the-Go Prayer

Let me set the scene for the idea of "On-the-Go Prayer." It's a story about Nehemiah.

Disobedient Israel has gone into captivity. Originally, it was Babylon, but the Medo-Persian Empire later conquered the Babylonians, so they are in power when this story takes place. Nehemiah has just discovered that the Holy City (Jerusalem) and the Temple itself is still in shambles. He is very upset, and enters the presence of the reigning king of that empire when the king notices his unhappy demeanor:

"The king asked, 'Well, how can I help you?' *With a prayer to the God of heaven, I replied*, 'If it please the king, and if you are pleased with me, your servant, send me to Judah to rebuild the city where my ancestors are buried.'"

Nehemiah 2:4-5 (NLT)

Nehemiah had come into the presence of the king in a sad frame of mind, having just discovered the dismal state of Jerusalem and the Temple. The king had never seen Nehemiah sad. Scholars say that servants of the king are never to enter his presence with sadness, with the possible penalty of death. So Nehemiah was taking a huge chance here—with his own life.

Notice that as soon as the king asked him what was wrong, Nehemiah shot a prayer off under his breath, sort of like me saying, "Help me, Lord," before answering. His plan worked. The King offered to help, asked how long he would be gone, and then even gave Nehemiah a blank check to cover the costs and guarantee his safe travel! So… "under your breath" prayers work, too! Start every new endeavor with prayer.

Lord, forgive me for thinking in the past that I didn't have time for prayer. Remind me that there's always time for prayer. In Jesus's name, amen.

Inspiration and Revelation

"*I pray that* the glorious Father, the *God* of our Lord Jesus Christ, would *give you a spirit of wisdom and revelation* as you come to know Christ better. Then you will have deeper insight. You will know the confidence that he calls you to have and the glorious wealth that God's people will inherit."

Ephesians 1:17-18 (GWT)

Have you ever read the Bible, seen something that struck you, and said, "Wow! I never noticed that before!" Guess what. It was there all along. This happened to me one day, and I realized that I needed to pray for that so it would happen more.

Here's the prayer I used when I began studying the Bible in my research for *My Search for the Real Heaven*.

Lord, You know what you meant when you wrote this; please help me to know what you mean as I read it. (I'm looking for heaven.) In Jesus's name, amen.

Then I noticed this verse, which seemed to verify that understanding and application of that understanding (wisdom) do not happen automatically; they are gifts from the Lord:

"Moses summoned all the Israelites and said to them, '**You have seen with your own eyes** everything the Lord did in the land of Egypt to Pharaoh and to all his servants and to his whole country—all the great tests of strength, the miraculous signs, and the amazing wonders. *But to this day the Lord has not given you minds that understand, nor eyes that see, nor ears that hear!*'"

Deuteronomy 29:2-4 (NLT)

Wait a minute. Are you telling me that unless God enables you, you can't really even see or hear or know or understand the big picture of what's going on right in front of you? Yes. Here's another verse confirming it:

"Ears to hear and eyes to see—both are gifts from the Lord."

Proverbs 20:12 (NLT)

After I discovered this I decided the only way to be able to see what's really going on all around me was to ask God to open my eyes, ears, heart, and mind to it. So here's my prayer:

Lord, please open my eyes, ears, heart, and mind to how You are at work all around me. Grant me inspiration and revelation. Forgive me for how in the past I've made decisions of what I wanted to do for the kingdom and then asked You to bless what I had planned—when what I should have been doing was asking You to show me how and where You are already at work; then joining that work. Forgive me for that arrogance. I guess Noah could have decided that he wanted to build a church building, but Your plans for a coming flood and the building of a boat were more important at the time. Remind me, Lord, that You are the Master, and that I am the servant; but a very blessed servant, who has been adopted into Your family. In Jesus's name, amen.

Praying for the Sick

"Are any of you *sick?* You should *call for the elders of the church to come and pray over you, anointing you with oil* in the name of the Lord."

James 5:14 (NLT)

This is a pet peeve of mine, so let me apologize up front if my thoughts here appear to be ... ranting and raving.

All my life I've listened to announcements and prayer requests at church for those who are sick or are facing serious surgery or long-term illness. Then the man would pray for these people. That's great, but I haven't felt their power—or more accurately, God's power—being called into play; sort of like the King who only asked the medical experts for help, leaving God out.

Obviously, by praying publicly, God isn't being left out, but the words usually repeated might as well have done that. Let me explain; here's what the prayer usually requests:

"Lord, Brother (or Sister) So-and-so is sick. Be with them. Bless the doctors and nurses and all the medicines used. Now, guide, guard, and direct us until the next appointed time."

Now I hate to criticize anyone's prayer, and please forgive me in advance if what I say next is offensive in any way, but here are my thoughts:

"Be with them." If I was God, I think I would say, "I'm already with them. And they're sick. What do you want me to do, child? Isn't there more you want from Me besides just 'being with them?'"

If we were having a two-way conversation then I would say, *"Oh, yeah. Please heal them."* "Okay," God might reply, "now we're getting somewhere. I can do that."

Or not. God does say no on occasion. But if we don't have, isn't it because we don't ask?

> "You want what you don't have, so you commit murder. You're determined to have things, but you can't get what you want. You quarrel and fight. *You don't have the things you want, because you don't pray for them.*"
>
> James 4:2 (GWT)

Of course, your requests are fueled by your motives, and God knows your motives; He knows exactly why you ask what you ask. If your motivation is self-centered and self-serving in nature, this prayer isn't a license to make God your own personal Santa in the sky. If, however, your motivation is pure; in the best interest of the kingdom, it's basically a blank check from God for whatever you need.

Who would think of sending soldiers into battle without providing every single thing they need to help them complete their mission.

You are on a mission—for God. He never promised to give you more than you need, but He did promise to provide everything you need. Keep that in mind, and let it bring you peace. If it brings glory to His kingdom—especially if non-Christians are watching—the person will be healed. But remember, healing and death can both bring God glory.

> *Lord, _____ is sick. Please heal them. Until You say, "No," I will pray for healing. I pledge to adjust my prayers based on what happens next. If you heal them I will praise You and tell all others. If you let them die, I will still praise You, help to comfort the family, and look for ways You are glorified by the circumstances. Grant me wisdom in my responses and my prayers. In Jesus's name, amen.*

Private (Closet) Prayers

"The eyes of the Lord watch over those who do right, and his ears are open to their prayers."

1 Peter 3:12a (NLT)

God listens. He hears every prayer. As discussed earlier, prayers can be hindered if you aren't in good standing with Him because of ongoing sin in your life, personal refusal of His grace, or not being in covenant with Him at all. But other than that, He has chosen prayer as the method ongoing relationship.

But God really, really listens to the requests from folks who are focused on doing right, obeying Him, expanding His kingdom. That's special—and should be a great encouragement. Are you doing right? Are you focused on building your kingdom, or His? Are you trying to bring the sweet aroma of Christ into everyday life? Then he really, really listens to you.

Though prayer is often a public event for the corporate body of Christ (the church), Jesus warned about public prayers. He warned us not to say words or phrases just for show. He doesn't want our public prayers to be robotic rituals of rote rants that are repeated randomly and don't come from our hearts:

> "Two men *went to the Temple to pray*. One was a Pharisee, and the other was a despised tax collector. *The Pharisee stood by himself and prayed* this prayer: 'I thank you, God, that I am not a sinner like everyone else. For I don't cheat, I don't sin, and I don't commit adultery. I'm certainly not like that tax collector! I fast twice a week, and I give you a tenth of my income.' But the tax collector stood at a distance and dared not even lift his eyes to heaven as he prayed. Instead, he beat his chest in sorrow, saying, 'O God, be merciful to me, for I am a sinner.' I tell you, this sinner, not the Pharisee, returned home justified before God. For

those who exalt themselves will be humbled, and those who humble themselves will be exalted."

Luke 18:10-14 (NLT)

The Pharisee had apparently stood in a prominent place in the Temple and prayed a loud prayer announcing his good deeds for everyone to hear. It didn't help him. The prayer had no effect at all in helping his standing with God. Prideful public prayers don't ever help anyone.

Jesus recommended private prayer in places of solitude— like closets:

"When you pray, don't be like the hypocrites who love to pray publicly on street corners and in the synagogues where everyone can see them. I tell you the truth, that is all the reward they will ever get. But *when you pray, go away by yourself, shut the door behind you, and pray to your Father in private.* Then your Father, who sees everything, will reward you."

Matthew 6:5-6 (NLT)

Motive is another problem. It's discussed in James 4. Do you have a motive problem? Are your prayers focused on getting what you want? Getting God to do your bidding? God knows your motives:

"For we speak as messengers approved by God to be entrusted with the Good News. Our purpose is to please *God*, not people. *He alone examines the motives of our hearts.*"

1 Thessalonians 2:4 (NLT)

Make sure your prayers are not just self-serving:

"What is causing the quarrels and fights among you? Don't they come from the *evil desires at war within you? You want what you don't have,* so you scheme and kill to get it. *You are jealous* of what others have, but you can't get it, so you fight and wage war to take it away from them. Yet you don't have what you want because you don't ask God for it. And even *when you ask, you don't get it because your motives are all wrong—you want only what will give you pleasure.*"

James 4:1-3 (NLT)

Lord, please forgive me for all my self-serving prayers in times past. In Jesus's name, amen.

Either / Or Prayers

"*God called you to do good, even if it means suffering*, just as Christ suffered for you. He is your example, and you must follow in his steps."

1 Peter 2:21 (NLT)

This one is a little confusing, but I felt like my thoughts here would bless others, so I decided to include it.

When I suffer, when I seemed bogged down and God appears unresponsive, the first thing to realize is that my own sin—which separates me from God's protection and healing—could possibly the reason for my suffering.

I already discussed the fact that your prayers can be hindered by physical objects and by bad habits and by sins. I am human, right? I fall back into old sin habits that I hoped I had broken, don't you? So when my prayers appear to be going unanswered, I have learned to pray my little "Either/Or" prayers. They go something like this (adapt this idea to your own circumstances):

Lord, I don't feel like I have an answer from You yet on the issue of _____. I don't want to reject it or move on with that issue until I know what You want. You might not be giving me an answer because I'm already where you want me. If that's the case, then give me the strength, courage, and patience to stay the course and finish this mission. However, if sin in my life—that I may be blind to—is keeping You from answering me, then please reveal my sin to me so I can repent, change, and draw near again to You. So, Lord, with respect, I ask You to either show me my sin, lead me in a new direction, or let me know somehow that I'm still on the path (the kingdom mission) You want me on for now. In Jesus's name, amen.

Sometimes, however, we are allowed to suffer for a season for the sake of the kingdom. So I sometimes add this:

Lord, I also realize that it's possible that I must suffer for now in my current situation. If You have chosen me for this, then I want to thank You for counting me worthy to suffer, and also ask that in my suffering I can praise You and bring You and Your kingdom great glory. In Jesus's name, amen.

Innovative Prayer Evangelism Ideas

The following is a list of fourteen evangelistic prayer ideas that I've heard used or read about over the years. Or at least these are the ones that were good enough to stick in my head. You might just try one or two; they are only suggestions. Every congregation is different and we all have different personalities. Some of them may work where you worship, others won't. But for goodness sake, do something!

1. Prayer Request Cards

This one is simple and cheap. Just keep prayer request cards available and within easy reach of any member or visitor. Let it be known they can be signed or unsigned. But if you do this be sure to convey that these requests will actually be honored. There are many ways to accomplish this. You can take them up at the beginning of the service, have someone copy them for follow up later, and then pour them out on the stage during the closing song, inviting members to come forward and get one to pray for that week. You can put the requests in the bulletin. You can announce it. How you do it best varies—mainly on the size of your congregation. But just do it.

You can also take this to a new level with "Prayer Grams," or some such name. These would be available to members and everyone would be encouraged to take them as needed. You can be quite creative with these. Pick some key people; Bible class teachers, small group leaders, and ladies class coordinators, and get them to brainstorm together about how to be most effective in promoting prayer in every possible way throughout the congregation.

2. Pray the Phone Book

Take the phone book from your city or community. Tear it up into individual pages. (You can also take it and have the binder cut off with an electronic paper cutter like printers use.) Distribute the individual pages of names throughout the church—to everyone willing to pray for those people by name. A prayer something like this:

> Lord, I pray right now for John Doe and his family at 1990 Southcastle. I pray that every individual in that family will be led to see their need for Jesus Christ because of the sin in their life. In Jesus's name, amen.

3. Have a Bible class with a Prayer Focus

The disciples asked Jesus to teach them to pray. So should we. You never get better at something until you talk about it, focus on it, and practice. Hold hands, go around the room and let each person pour out their heart. No hurry. You'll be surprised what people will pray for and you'll be encouraged. Most of all, you'll get a lot of experience—first-hand and second-hand. Let it soak in. Really listen. Don't worry if there are long moments of silence;

just relax and let it come. Mingle a few verses and shared experiences in, and it's a recipe for success—prayer success.

4. Consider a Once a Month Prayer Service

Let everyone in the church know ahead of time exactly what you will do. Then ask every family to bring at least one person. Ideally, get each individual to bring one. But start small, make the goals reachable, and begin. Just do it.

The service needs to focus on prayer. Nothing else. Distribute cards ahead of time so members and friends can share them with others. Make it a regular monthly thing, and watch it grow. People will eventually see it as a loving act of kindness; everyone needs prayer for something. The trick is getting people to understand you're truly interested in their and their personal needs. It will grow. God will help you.

You might eventually even want to make this event a weekly thing. I visited one church in a big city that began a Tuesday night prayer service. The first week there were two. It grew every week. They now have over 5,000 people every single Tuesday night. God loves to hear from us.

5. Community Prayer Groups

Some have begin having interfaith community prayer meetings in a public place like the city library. Make it regular; invite every preacher in the area; have the put it in their announcements. Let it be known that the focus will be to pray in unity together for community issues: crime, local leaders, first responders, etc. This is sure to open all sorts of ministry opportunities. Pray for God's lead in this. Every community has specific parts of town with more problems. Do prayer walks as a group. Assign blocks of prayer walk partners to pray for specific areas until the next monthly group meeting. You get the idea; be creative and open to God's nudges all along the way. Don't be hard and fast; strict rules up front will limit involvement and build walls, and your goal here is to tear those walls down and build the kingdom up. You can even visit community leaders like the Mayor or City Council members and ask what they want your group to pray for specifically. Everyone needs prayer for something.

6. Door Hangers

You can purchase inexpensive door hanger flyers that can be preprinted as prayer request cards. If you promote this properly throughout your church, you can get each member to hang the blank cards on some doors in their neighborhoods. Put them out on maybe Thursday, print on it that you'll gather them up on Saturday evening, and people will pray for them on Sunday. They will still get prayer even if they don't want their name on the request. Make people comfortable with sharing—whatever it takes.

7. Pray Over the Visitors Chairs

I read once about a church that hadn't baptized but one hundred people in the last ten years. A small group of prayer warriors decided to pray regularly over each chair on the back row—the place visitors always sat. They would touch each seat individually and pray this prayer:

> Lord, please send a lost soul to this seat. When they get here, open their eyes, ears, heart, and mind to the truth of the gospel of Jesus Christ. Help them to see their own sin and realize their need to be saved. In Jesus's name, amen.

They moved from chair to chair and repeated the same words. They baptized one hundred that year. God is still on the throne, and prayer still works.

8. Parking-Lot Prayer

This idea is a little more aggressive and bold, but every congregation has someone with the personality to do it—if they are kingdom-focused and willing. Practice and pray before you begin trying it, and I can guarantee this will make an unforgettable impression on visitors.

Stand by the visitors' parking spots in the parking lot before service. When a visitor parks and gets out, walk up with a friendly smile and offer a welcome handshake. Thank them for coming, express your hope they enjoy their visit, and ask if they have any prayer need. Everyone has a prayer need or two, and many will tell you what it is if you'll simply ask. After all, they are visitor, and they showed up today for a reason, right? It's that simple. The following conversation is offered to get you to think about possibilities and approaches:

"Hi, folks, welcome to our church. Thank you for coming today. Enjoy the worship. By the way, is there anything you need prayed for?"

"Well, my wife, Susie, has a grandmother who she is very close to, and she's in ICU right now."

"Okay, let's pray. *Dear God, please bless Susie and this family as they deal with the emotional strain of having a loved one in ICU with her life in the balance. You made us, Lord, and You can fix our damaged bodies when they won't work right anymore. We pray for healing. We pray for comfort. We pray for peace. We pray that good things can come from this difficult situation, and when they do, Lord, remind us that it was You who caused it. Also bless the doctors, nurses, and medicines. In Jesus's name, amen.*"

"Again, folks, thanks for coming today. Enjoy the service— and come back sometime!"

They'll be back (as Arnold would say).

9. Specific Circumstance Prayer

This suggestion requires a background story. I'm using fictitious names for obvious reasons.

Bob was a school official and Sue worked in the home taking care of their children. Sue's brother, Jim, had lived a life of faith for many years, growing up in a Christian home, accepting

Christ, and being actively involved in church. But sadly, something clicked in Jim's heart, and turned his back on God and his church friends. He shunned them in every possible way, living instead like people of the world rather than a man of faith. Sue had prayed for Jim's return for years. Nothing.

Then one day Sue changed her prayer. This is what she said:

"Lord, I will do whatever it takes for Jim to come back to you."

When you examine it and think about it, that's quite an audacious prayer. It communicates a willing heart as a soldier for the king that's willing to sacrifice in order to accomplish a beneficial outcome. Impressive. Committed. Focused. Earnest.

It got God's attention. Here's what happened.

The very next month, Bob was caught kissing one of the teachers at the school where he worked. Apparently, they were on the verge of an affair (a nice word for adultery), but backed off and ended the relationship as a result of getting caught. (This was likely the best possible thing for Bob's eternal soul.)

The couple separated for a while, got Christian counseling, worked out their problems (every marriage has them), and reconciled.

Jim watched the whole thing unfold, came to his senses, and returned to a life of faith.

Now I'm pretty sure that Sue would never have thought to pray, *"Lord, please help Bob to almost have an affair so we can reconcile, bring Jim back into the church."* But God knew the exact circumstances that would make that happen, and it just happed to be that Bob's plans needed to be uncovered, saving Jim and Bob—and the whole family—from years of pain, financial hardship, and much heartache. God is good.

After I learned of that story, I came up with a prayer that fits, and I share it with you here and now:

> *Lord, I am praying for John. You know exactly what circumstances will make that happen. So I'm praying for You to*

orchestrate the circumstances that will bring John to a realization of his sins and his need for You. In Jesus's name, amen.

10. Random Prayer

You've heard of, "Random acts of kindness." I want you to consider, "Random acts of prayer."

When you see someone on the side of the road looking sad or upset, pray. Just pray. *"Lord,"* you can say, *"give that person what they need most. You know what that is. In Jesus's name, amen."*

I do it all the time now. I can't wait to hear the stories from these folks in heaven some day about what God did in their lives after I prayed for them!

11. A Wake-Up Prayer

Lord, thank you for the new day and the night's rest. Thank you for your watchful care in the night while I slept. Now, what can I do for the kingdom today? ...

12. A Five-Part Prayer

I pray this prayer often:
Lord, help me to be Your man (or woman), doing Your will in Your way with Your attitude and Your timing. In Jesus's name, amen."

Submissive, obedient, and godly in approach, attitude, and timing. Five parts.

I think if I am on target with all five of these, I'm pretty much on the right track, right?

Moses had it all right at age forty except the timing, didn't he? He was forty years off.

Jonah had it all right except the attitude. In fact, when God forgave the people of Nineveh, Jonah was mad. Furious. In fact, he said, "Just kill me." He was so prejudiced that he preferred death over life in a world with forgiven Ninevehities. That's bad.

So attitude and timing are last, but vitally important. Never forget that. It helps when your prayer answers seem delay d. God is patient, so work to be more like Him every day.

13. Creative Prayer

Brothers and sisters, be creative. Ask God what to pray about. Ask God who to pray for. Ask for others to pray for you. Don't let pride stop you from doing this. Share your fears with close Christian friends. Listen for His gentle nudges. Yearn for His presence. Seek His guidance. Trust that He will provide. Draw closer and closer to Him. He loves you.

Deliver Us from Evil

"Lead us not into temptation, but *deliver us from evil.*"

Matthew 6:13a (KJV)

This was an important part of the prayer Jesus taught His disciples when they asked Him to teach them to pray.

Evil abounds. Morals are declining. Bible knowledge is becoming a thing of the past. Youth Ministers often teach more drama, puppet skits, and fluffy stories than they do Bible verses. Look at the curriculum from any church and see? Evil runs rampant. Does anyone doubt this? Then go back to the first chapter and review the Ephesians 6 discussion.

Do you want to be delivered from evil? I do. Pray for it.

I don't mean to scare folks with this possibility, but … evil doesn't exist only outside churches. The Bible warns continually of false prophets and false teachers.

> "There used to be false prophets among God's people, just as *you will have some false teachers in your group.* They will secretly teach things that are wrong—teachings that will cause people to be lost."
>
> 2 Peter 2:1a

Lord, I pray just what you taught the disciples to pray: please deliver me from evil. Protect me from evil. Open my eyes to evil. Give me discernment concerning the evil all around me— even among those who I attend worship with. And then give me the courage to reject evil in every possible way in my daily life. In Jesus's name, amen.

Don't Bless Me TOO Much

"God, have mercy on us and **bless us** and show us your kindness."

Psalm 67:1 (NCV)

This prayer might sound a little strange, but please bear with me—I think it's important.

We are trained from early on that we need blessings from God. We need His help. He loves us very much and wants to see us grow and prosper. But financial prosperity—while essential for living, taking care of our families, and giving generously to others—is very often a trap used by Satan to get us to take our focus of the Giver (God) to the gifts (all the blessings). It's a very dangerous possibility that we must be keenly aware of.

In light of this threat, I pray this prayer, and offer it for you to consider:

Lord, please bless me with all I can handle and still be faithful to You. I don't want one penny more than that—whatever that number is. I don't want to gain the whole world if it costs me my soul. And, Lord, You know exactly where that threshold is. Stop me before I go over that cliff. Keep in in check in this area of my life. I trust You to know that. In Jesus's name, amen.

Demon Epilog

I didn't jump. And I did my best to forget that experience and that day. But as I grew in the knowledge of God and in my Bible study of demons in scripture, that experience came back to mind like an old enemy.

Now that I've left the world of business and entered the world of ministry, writing, speaking, and traveling all over the world to get people excited about God and heaven, I hear stories from others (and had other experiences myself) that make me realize how active Satan is in his efforts to a) lead us away from God, and b) focus on people at strategic moments in their lives to thwart the good they will do.

By that I don't mean that Satan knows the future, because only God knows every detail of our future. But I do think that Satan and his forces work diligently to stop the plans of God in people's life as their direction begins to unfold, making it more and more obvious that the light of the kingdom of God is shining through those individuals. When that light gets brighter, Satan works to put it out. Quickly and thoroughly.

How about you? Is your light shining brighter for God? If so, Satan is noticing you, so you will become more and more of a target. But don't worry; He that is in us (God's Holy Spirit) is greater than he that is in the world (Satan). Be aware of the battle, but be reminded that you already have victory through Christ. Now let's talk a little more about Spiritual Warfare and how you can win your daily battles through prayer and knowledge of the things of God. Join me as I describe the great struggles I have faced as a Christian in the world of business, and a few friends who have done the same. Let's learn from each other. We Christians are comrades in arms. Iron sharpens iron, so let's all sharpen our skills by sharing our victories—and defeats.

Lord, thank You for the fact that I did not jump that day. Thank You for somehow stopping me. From now on, help me to be deaf to Satan and his forces against me and help me to have open ears to Your messages to me. And once I know Your message give me a willing heart to obey. What can I do for the Kingdom today?